BILLION CODES

The Codes that Billionaire Use to Create Wealth that Others Don't

Dr. Stephen Akintayo

CONTENTS

PART SEVENTEEN: LOVE CODE

Chapter 27: Emotional Intelligence

INTRODUCTION
THE BILLIONAIRE CODES

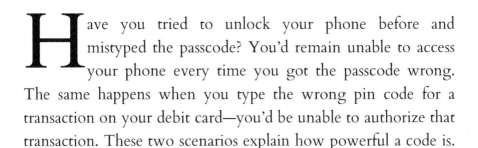

Have you tried to unlock your phone before and mistyped the passcode? You'd remain unable to access your phone every time you got the passcode wrong. The same happens when you type the wrong pin code for a transaction on your debit card—you'd be unable to authorize that transaction. These two scenarios explain how powerful a code is. It can determine whether you get access or not. It determines if a transaction will be successful or not.

Billionaires, too, have codes with which they unlock their wealth or riches. It doesn't just happen. These codes are principles or laws that govern wealth creation and multiplication. These codes grant them access to many doors of wealth and success that make them outstanding and the envy of all eyes. Becoming wealthy is not magic, it answers to principles.

This book is a sequel to *The Billionaire Habits* where I explained the habits that help Billionaires create their wealth. What I have done with this book is to expose you to *the codes that govern those habits*. Picture the codes a the building blocks of each habit. Understanding these codes is like having the keys that help you access the doors that lead to wealth and success.

It's a delight to have you journey together with me once again. I believe it will be a worthwhile experience and I look forward to hearing stories of your wealth and success as a result of applying these codes.

PEOPLE CODE

Is there a code for understanding people and working with them to achieve your goals? Absolutely! It is one of the secret codes of billionaires. The *people code* shows that people equal money. People are assets that every billionaire has in abundance.

Billionaires prioritize people above money because they know that people can generate money, but money cannot generate people. Therefore, they place a high premium on people than they do on money. They know that the more valuable the people working for them and helping them in various aspects of life and business are, the more likely to succeed they are. Chapters 1 – 5 border on relationships—*mutually beneficial, result oriented, visionary, honest and positive relationships.* At the end of this part, you would have realized how important your associations are to wealth creation and maintenance.

CHAPTER ONE

MUTUALLY BENEFICIAL
RELATIONSHIPS

"Your network plays a significant role in your financial attainment."

– Dr. Stephen Akintayo

Years ago, my family and I used to live in a suburban part of Lagos State, Nigeria. We were living an average, comfortable life by the standards of the day. But eventually, God started blessing me and I began to travel outside the country and all of a sudden people started paying attention to me and my family. It got to a point that the attention we were receiving in the community was unnecessary and started to make us feel uncomfortable. I recall how on several occasions when I returned from a journey, it was the commercial motorcycle operators (popularly known as Okada men) in the community who would sight me from a distance and quickly run to inform my wife that I have returned from my journey. Eventually, it began to look as if we were the ones in the entire community who traveled more often. As a result, I had to tell my wife that it was time to leave that neighborhood. I said to her, "We cannot continue to live in this neighborhood and look as if we are the richest. That is not a good omen. It is better we move to a new place where we will be challenged."

"Your environment, your network of influence, and your social circles are important factors to consider when it comes to making wealth. The fact is your network plays a significant role in your financial attainment."

My idea was to move to a place where what we had would be considered as nothing by members of that community. In that way, we would be challenged to do more and achieve more. And that was what happened. I remember how after moving to our new location, I woke up the following day and stood by the balcony of our story-building and upon glancing at my neighbor's compound to the right and seeing the types of cars he had, I suddenly realized that the least of his cars was ten times better in value than my only good car. Just to be sure, I looked to

my neighbor's cars to the left and the story was the same. Then I thought to myself, "Yes, we have made the right decision. We have moved to the right environment. Now we will hustle and work hard to climb up." And that eventually happened. By merely moving to a new location, we were consciously challenged to work harder than before in order to meet up the social expectations of our environment. As I am writing this, we are already considering moving to a new location where we will be more challenged than where we currently are. We may be moving to Banana Island in the next couple of months, who knows?

I shared this personal anecdote to make the point that your environment, your network of influence, and your social circles are important factors to consider when it comes to making wealth. The fact is your network plays a significant role in your financial attainment. This is one of the secrets of billionaires.

Are Rich People Arrogant?

Years ago, I used to think that every rich person is arrogant and proud. I dare to say that this is typically how poor people think about rich people. They assume that rich people like to show off their wealth; don't want to associate with people not in their class; and do not consider poor people as anything. Well,

"If you are the only rich person where you are, you are poor."

as I said, I used to think that way too. As a matter of fact, the more I began to associate with rich people the more I realized that a lot of them are humble and simple. I dare to say that some of the humblest people you will ever meet are among the rich. But before you crucify, holding that it's because I am now rich, permit me to explain certain things to you. And in case you know me personally and think that way about me, give me a few moments to explain some secrets to you.

If you are the only rich person where you are, you are poor. If everybody surrounding you is poor, it does not matter the amount of money you have or how wealthy you think you are, you are still poor. The reason is that everyone around you will be bothering you with their problems and you will be busy solving all their problems to the extent that you might end up losing the money that you have acquired over the years. Hence, it is important to share the secrets of wealth with others so that they too can learn these habits and be better off.

You cannot be rich by having poor habits. For example, if you develop the habit of always associating with people who are like you or worse than you are, you should not expect to grow

exponentially in that kind of situation. The adage, "Show me your friend and I will tell you who you are," is rightly applicable to this kind of situation. Don't aspire to be the one-eyed man in the city of the blind just so that you can shine and feel good about yourself. The reality is that if you are always the brightest or the best among your friends, then something is wrong. It's high time you changed that network and moved on because if you don't, your life will be stagnated, and you won't make any reasonable progress in life.

The point must be pellucidly made that if you love to associate with people who lack focus or have a poverty mentality, you will invariably become like them. Unfortunately, because of low self-esteem, many people choose friends who are worse than they are just so they can feel important about themselves. The idea is that if they associate with people whose socioeconomic conditions are worse than theirs, people with a mediocre mindset, then they will feel good about themselves since others will see them as the shining light. Such people will never want to associate with others who are better than them just to protect their ego from being punctured. That is a faulty and mediocre philosophy of life. There are many problems with this kind of thinking.

First, if you are always the brightest among the people with whom you associate, then something is fundamentally wrong. Anytime you discover that you are the brightest among all your friends and they always run to you to solve their problems, but you cannot look up to them to help you with your struggles, it is time to run away from them or at least tactically dissociate yourself from them and find yourself a new set of friends who will challenge and spur you to reach your potentials. Any relationship that is not mutually beneficial is parasitical. You must be conscious to build relationships that are not only symbiotic but also reciprocal.

"if you are always the brightest among the people with whom you associate, then something is fundamentally wrong."

Second, if you are rich and, in the guise of humility, you continue to associate with poor people, you will soon start thinking like them and eventually lose the fortune that you have worked hard over the years to acquire. Association influences. Gone are the days when we thought peer pressure only affected children and teenagers. The reality is that peer pressure follows us throughout every stage of our lives. Admittedly, some groups (like teenagers) are more susceptible to succumbing to peer pressures than others. But we are all influenced by our

environment more than we can imagine. In his groundbreaking book, *The Tipping Point,* Malcolm Gladwell makes the case that our social environment is contagious more than we usually want to imagine. Hence, when rich people decide to associate with poor people, they will begin to pick up their habits, and eventually, everyone in that social circle will become poor. But when this scenario plays out the other way around, the poor person stands to benefit a lot from the rich and there are higher chances that he or she will move towards becoming rich.

Third, it appears that the third law of motion is what is practically at play in the way poor people often think about rich people. Because of the wrong, general assumption that rich people must have done something bad or mischievous to acquire riches, it is not unlikely for poor people to resent them even without meeting or knowing them. Since "for every action, there is always an equal and an opposite reaction," it follows that rich people are often attracted to people of their caliber or those who are wealthier than them, and poor people cannot but think of rich people as acting in braggadocious ways.

Today, I can confidently tell you that while there are some rich people that are arrogant and proud, the majority of them are not. It may shock you to realize that most rich people are humbler than a lot of poor people. I know you may want to dispute this, but that is a given. I am speaking from my personal experience

and from my observations in my dealings and interactions with rich people. Most billionaires are less judgmental, less racist, and more open-minded than most poor people. Suffice it to say that it took me a while to realize these things that I am sharing with you. The point of the matter is that billionaires only go for mutually beneficial relationships. Come to think of it, if a relationship is not going to mutually benefit you, why go into it? In other words, why start a relationship with anyone who is not going to add value to your life?

I used to think that rich people are so arrogant that they would not want to relate with me. But over the years, I continue to be shocked and surprised anytime rich and highly placed people in society reach out to me telling me they got my phone number from so and so person. In most of those instances, these are people I have been thinking and wishing I would have the privilege to connect with in the future. To my amazement, it is these same people who are humble enough to reach out to me. Why do you think this is so? It is because they know that our relationship is going to be

mutually beneficial. They know that I have something that I can add to them and of course they have something to add to me. If I have not worked hard to be in a position where I can add value to society, such people would not even know that someone like me exists not to talk of reaching out to me.

"The point of the matter is that billionaires only go for mutually beneficial relationships. Come to think of it, if a relationship is not going to mutually benefit you, why go into it?"

My point is that billionaires only become friends with mutually beneficial people. Yes, I know I am rich, but how can you also add value to my life? How useful are you to me? These are some of the questions that always run through the mind of billionaires. I can assure you that if billionaires know that you have some value that you can add to them, even if you are not in their socioeconomic class, they will not feel drawn to reach out to you. This is one of the major secrets of billionaires. And I think this totally makes sense because if billionaires have not always associated with people who add value to them, how would they have been that wealthy?

Conversely, this is one of the major problems of poor people. Most poor people befriend other poor people just for the sake of friendship without thinking about the value they derive from or add to the other person. You become friends with people who have never touched your life in any way and from every standpoint they have nothing to contribute to making your life

better. They can only take away value from you. They are the ones who are always saying bad things about you to others, looking for every opportunity to gossip and blackmail you, seeing you as a rival or competitor, and in some worse scenarios, they may betray or connive to harm you. Yet, you know these things and still want to associate with such people.

Tell me, why would rich people waste their time in such vain pursuits? Rich people are preoccupied with a lot of things that if they decide to spend five minutes with you, they have already done their math and arrived at the conclusion that those five minutes are going to benefit them.

Who are your friends? How much value are they adding to your life? People either take from you or add to you. If you want to create wealth and have a lot of riches, you must always aim for mutually beneficial relationships — relationships where

"Most poor people befriend other poor people just for the sake of friendship without thinking about the value they derive from or add to the other person."

they take from you, yet add to you; you give to them, yet take from them. Stop wasting your time trying to mingle with or working so hard to please people that are not adding value to you.

Think Win/Win

Amutually bebeficial relationship can be described in the words of Stephen R. Covey, the author of one of the best books ever written on personal development, *The 7 Habits of Highly Effective People,* as a Win/Win relationship. According to Covey, the most effective interpersonal skill anyone can have is to think Win/Win. "Win-Win is a frame of mind and heart that constantly seeks mutual benefit in all human interactions," Covey wrote. He went on to say, "Win/Win means that agreement or solutions are mutually beneficial, mutually satisfying. With a Win/Win solution, all parties feel good about the decision and feel committed to the action plan." One of the most profound things Covey says about this philosophy is that "Win/Win sees life as a cooperative, not a competitive arena." Because billionaires understand this principle, this is one of the major principles they operate with.

Unfortunately, many poor people usually strive for Win/Lose, Lose/Win, or the worst of all, Lose/Lose philosophy.

Most poor people's relationships can be categorized as a Lose/Lose scenario in that they are not gaining anything of value from their social circles neither are those people deriving anything of benefit from the relationship. They're comfortable that way: "You're not better than me, I'm not better than you. As long as you're not better than me, we're fine." In the end, you have millions of people who are actively engaged in social interactions that are nothing but a waste of time and energy. This is the reason entire communities may end up becoming poor from one generation to another without anyone breaking the vicious circle to do something meaningful that will change the narrative.

A Win/Win attitude is a mutually beneficial relationship attitude.Under this situation, you make progress and I make progress; you add value to me, and I add value to you; you complement my weaknesses while I also complement yours. This is how mutually beneficial relationships work. In a situation where people only want to gain from you without contributing anything to you, they become nothing less than parasites who are out to destroy you.

> *"The idea of OQP entails relating, interacting, and associating only with people who have been tested and proven to be reliable, valuable, and relatable."*

But someone may say, "I am poor, how then can I add value to someone who is already influential? Why wouldn't that person just help me to come out of my predicament so that I too can help others?" The fact is that in the real world, nothing goes for nothing. And I think this is one of the foundational problems of poor people and the reason why many of them remain perpetually poor and end up resenting rich people for what they often term as 'greed' or 'selfishness.'

To think that you must be rich or have something very important before you can be in a mutually beneficial relationship is one of the greatest lies of all times. Let me give you a practical example: I do a lot of free teaching on my social media handles to give back to the community and add value to others. As a matter of fact, I taught most of the ideas in this book

"Until you adopt a Win/Win attitude in your relationships, you are bound to remain stagnant or backward in your socioeconomic state."

on my social media for free before converting it into a book. If you have been following me on any of my pages, one thing I always do is to ask my audience to help share my videos ten times, twenty times, fifty times, and so forth. The reason I do so is twofold. First, it is so that the value I am sharing may reach many people and benefit them. Second, it is my way of teaching you to reciprocate the value I am giving you.

Let me state a simple, known fact here: Sharing a video on social media does not cost anything. But guess what? Most people who watch or listen to my videos usually refuse to share them despite many pleas throughout the videos for them to do so. Isn't it mindboggling that people will consume your content for free but intentionally refuse to share it with others even after pleading with them to do so? How can such people who refuse to do something so little that will cost them nothing cultivate mutually beneficial relationships with rich people? It is all about the mindset. Most people who refuse to share videos with others despite knowing that doing so will not contribute anything significant to me (since I am already financially independent)

"A Win/Win attitude is a mutually beneficial relationship attitude. Under this situation, you make progress and I make progress; you add value to me, and I add value to you; you complement my weaknesses while I also complement yours."

erroneously think that if they share my content then they stand to lose while I stand to gain. But in reality, sharing free content that you find beneficial online is a Win/Win situation.

Until you adopt a Win/Win attitude in your relationships, you are bound to remain stagnant or backward in your socioeconomic state. Do you want to become a billionaire? Then start thinking of how to add value to others and how to derive value from them. Think Win/Win.

Practice Only Quality People

Another idea that is closely related to Win/Win philosophy that is particularly important to imbibe is to practice Only Quality People (OQP)—an idea that has been promulgated by the world-renowned motivational speaker, Les Brown. According to Brown, one of the attitudes for success is to practice OQP. The idea of OQP entails relating, interacting, and associating only with people who have been tested and proven to be reliable, valuable, and relatable. This is one of the secret habits of billionaires. If you must create wealth and acquire riches, you

must learn to weed off people in your life who do not contribute anything meaningful to you.

What benefits are there in relating with people who are always whining, gossiping, castigating others, and wasting your precious time with negative talks about others or certain events in the society? After meeting or talking with such people, you realize that no value has been added to you. Instead, you feel drained emotionally and spiritually because someone has succeeded in polluting your mind with negativity. The earlier you cut off such people from your life, the better it would be for you. You must embrace this philosophy and stand by it. If they cannot add value to your life, move on, never turn back, and never feel guilty about it.

The kind of people you want to surround yourself with are those that when they win, you win; when they make progress, you also make progress. You must be determined to cut off people who are always telling you, "Please help me," "Please save me," "Please change my life," "If you don't help me, I will die." Such people do not mean well for you. If you play into their chicaneries and subterfuges, you may discover your mistake when it is too late. Generally, such people are alarmists who will try to manipulate you by appealing to your emotions to see that their situation is dire and make you feel guilty if you refuse to do their biddings.

You must learn to discern such people and resist them. They do not fit into the category of OQP. Such people are better referred to as OPP (Only Poor People).

One of the ways to overcome the pressures OPP will want to put on you is to always remind them that everyone has a problem. And that is a fact. You also have a lot of problems that you are seeking solutions for. Isn't that what life is all about? We are all seeking a solution to something that will make our lives better. As we say in Nigeria, "*Wahala no dey finish*" (Trouble doesn't end). Such people must understand that everybody has a problem which they are trying to solve or overcome.

> "*The kind of people you want to surround yourself with are those that when they win, you win; when they make progress, you also make progress.*"

You have to be serious with the idea that anytime you are going into a relationship with someone you are determined to add value to them and, most importantly, you are sure that they are people who will add value to you. Let me share two real-life stories to buttress this point. The first story has to do with Pastor E. A. Adeboye (popularly known as Daddy G.O.), the General Overseer of the

Redeemed Christian Church of God (RCCG). He was once preaching at the Redemption Camp and said, "My son died." Since no one had heard of such a misfortune befalling the popular Man of God, people were immediately startled and stupefied. Since such large gatherings always involve an interpreter who interprets Daddy G.O.'s message from English to Yoruba, the interpreter on this occasion thought that Daddy G. O. had made a mistake and so instead of interpreting what he had said, he decided to keep quiet with the hope that the mistake would be corrected. So, Daddy G. O. had to repeat it. This time he said, "I said, my son died."

Given this scenario, the interpreter reluctantly and, most probably fearfully, interpreted the message. As if that was not enough, Daddy G. O. went on to say, "This my son is so dear to me. Every time I am in the United Kingdom, he comes around to handle my laundry, plan my itinerary, arrange my food, and do a lot of other things to help me." He continued, "The last time I was in the United Kingdom, he was in a hospital bed. I visited him to pray for him and he was concerned about who would take care of me that even while on a hospital bed he spoke with one of his friends and instructed him to be of help to me. I looked at him and told him he should not be concerned about my welfare, my desire and prayer for him is to be well." I am sure that you are wondering the relevance of this story to what we have been talking about. The lesson is simple: How many of you who know

Daddy G. O. would believe that a man of his caliber and status would cherish and be reminiscent of the services that someone offered him freely whereas if he needed hundreds of people to be paid to take care of him that wouldn't be an issue? That is exactly my point.

Many poor people think that rich and powerful people don't have any problems. They think to themselves, "I am the only one that has a problem.

". When you begin to think that everything is all about you and you don't pause to think about how to add value to others, you are practicing OPP instead of OQP. . When you begin to think that everything is all about you and you don't pause to think about how to add value to others, you are practicing OPP instead of OQP."

Everyone must try to help me. If they fail to help me, they are bad people." That is surely a selfish way of looking at life. When you begin to think that everything is all about you and you don't pause to think about how to add value to others, you are practicing OPP instead of OQP. Understand this: Every rich person has a problem or a need that they would appreciate the help another person is willing to give them, especially if such help does not have any strings attached. And God has structured life in such a way that most times the solutions to a rich man's problems are in the hands of the poor, and vice-versa. A rich man's major problems may not be money-related but most of a poor man's problems are money-related. So the rich man needs the poor man in the same way the poor man needs the rich man. But many times everyone is so engrossed with their problems that they don't think about the problems of another person and how they can possibly be the solution. That is our human nature.

The second story relates to my encounter with the Minister of Transportation in Nigeria. I was staying in a hotel and decided to take the elevator. Behold I discovered that I was in the elevator with the Minister. He was already in the elevator by the time I entered. I immediately recognized him and greeted him, and he also greeted me. But you could see that he was anxiously expecting me to present a request or ask a favor from him, which is the normal way that our people act when they accidentally encounter people who are occupying a political position, are influential, or powerful. They always want to take advantage of the situation by saying things like, "It was God that arranged this meeting. Thank God I met you. Kindly help me solve this problem or that." Of course, I can't deny that I had the urge to talk to him. And I definitely knew what kind of favor I could ask from a Minister of Transportation. But as I thought about it for a moment, I couldn't come up with anything that the man needed and how I could be of help to him.

"Every form of relationship, I believe, must be mutually beneficial. And that is how billionaires think."

Based on that, I didn't ask him for any favor. By the time he was coming out of the elevator, I could literally see the surprise on his face. I thought to myself, "Maybe this is the first time he is meeting someone who did not 'seize the opportunity' to ask him for a favor."

While someone may think that mine was a missed opportunity, I do not regret it. Every form of relationship, I believe, must be mutually beneficial. And that is how billionaires think. When a billionaire meets another billionaire, he does not start begging, "Please, help me. Kindly do this or that for me." Instead, he is always thinking, "How can I solve this guy's problem?" He may know what he needs from the other guy, but the first thing he is thinking about is, "What value can I add to his life so that our relationship will make sense?" And this is one of the powerful lessons about mutually beneficial relationships. Ask an average billionaire whom his closest friends are, and you will be amazed to discover that he has mutually beneficial business dealings with all of them. Among all my closest friends today, there is one form of business or the other that links us together. In fact, it was because of the business transaction that our relationship got closer, stronger, and better. Here's another practical example to explicate this point: Femi Otedola and Aliko Dangote, two of Nigeria's most influential business magnates and philanthropists, were always in the newspapers because of one squabble, altercation, or misunderstanding. But today the two of them are best of friends. Why do you think this is so? I don't have all the facts, but I can rightly conjecture that it is because they are engaged in business ventures together.

While billionaires build mutually beneficial relationships around their businesses, most poor people's relationships have little or nothing to do with business. The only thing that may be in the form of exchange among poor people is the lending and borrowing of money from one another. One of the reasons why poor people continue to remain poor is because they are not friends with many of the people with whom they carry out business transactions. Most times, even relatives of poor people, because of low self-esteem, only relate with their rich brothers and sisters when they need money. They will only call you to ask you to intervene to solve their financial woes. They don't act like friends or brothers and sisters who genuinely care about your welfare and would call you from time to time just to have a meaningful conversation with you or simply to check on your well-being. They only care about their own interest, that is, what they can gain from you. Such attitude is revolting. If someone did it to you, you'd hate it. Well, that's how another person would hate it too.

One of the aides to the current Vice President of Nigeria, Professor Yemi Osibanjo, expressed her grievances during a church program about such attitudes toward the rich and the powerful that corroborates the point I have been trying to make about the need to have mutually beneficial relationships.

"To create lasting wealth and maintain it, you must be determined to henceforth engage in mutually beneficial relationships."

She said, "Since my boss became the Vice President, everyone who calls him is always asking for one favor or the other. But we hardly have people call my boss to tell him that they have the solution to some of the problems of Nigeria. Hardly do people call him to add value to him. They are always calling him about their problems." She ended with saying, "This is part of the reason why Nigeria is not progressing." I concur with her sentiment. We see this everywhere in Africa. When a relative gets elected to a political office, everyone who knows him suddenly begins to feel that this is their turn to extort the government—their turn to have a share in the 'national cake.' Hardly do those friends and relatives say, "This is an opportunity for one of us to change the narrative in the country. What part can we play to help him make a change so that he will be remembered for good in the coming generations?"

To create lasting wealth and maintain it, you must be determined to henceforth engage in mutually beneficial relationships. If you apply this principle in your life, it will not be long before you begin to notice the difference in your mental outlook and income level—because association influences.

CHAPTER SUMMARY

- A mutually beneficial relationship, in a nutshell, is one where they take from you, yet add to you; you give to them, yet take from them. You must consciously build such relationships.
- A mutually beneficial relationship works by a win-win attitude where both parties compensate each other's weaknesses.
- What a billionaire thinks about first in a relationship with a fellow billionaire is how he can add value to the other person.
- Your environment, your network of influence, and your social circles are important factors to consider when it comes to making wealth. They play a significant role in your financial attainment.
- To create lasting wealth and maintain it, you must be determined to henceforth engage in mutually beneficial relationships.

CHAPTER 2

RESULT-ORIENTED RELATIONSHIPS

"You do not only need to have mutually beneficial relationships, but also result-oriented ones."

– Dr. Stephen Akintayo

Aside from going after mutually beneficial relationships, billionaires have learned from experience to focus their attention and energy on result-oriented relationships. What is a result-oriented relationship? It is a relationship that is built on the principle of goal attainment. Before

"What is a result-oriented relationship? It is a relationship that is built on the principle of goal attainment."

billionaires agree to engage in any relationship, they first examine the pros and cons of such a relational transaction. But they do not stop there. The next thing they do is try to project the kinds of goals the team is going to achieve in the near future. This is one of the secrets of wealth creation. You do not only need to have mutually beneficial relationships, but also result-oriented ones.

Result-oriented people have vision, mission, and goals in life. They don't have time to waste in pursuing aimless or goalless relationships. Such is the habit of billionaires.

Be Mindful of Your Associations

One of my friends, an American-based Nigerian, decided to visit his hometown in Nigeria after some time of living away from home. God has blessed him, and he is doing very well in the United States. As the expectation always is, his relations at home expected that he came with a lot of money and, of course, they were going to benefit from his good fortune. My friend was quite benevolent to his people during the visit. But specifically, he decided to give one of his uncles a lot of money. According to what he told me, sometime later after he returned to the United States, his leg began to swell up to the point that he had trouble walking around.

Since it was not long after he returned from Nigeria that he was struck with the ailment, his mother thought that the ailment must have something to do with his visit to the village. She decided to do some findings and what she discovered was heartbreaking and startling. The uncle who received a lot of money from her son arrogantly told her that he was responsible for her son's predicament. Can you guess the reason? According to him, it was because her son *insulted* him by giving him old dollar notes. In other words, he expected that his nephew would give him new dollar notes instead of old ones. Therefore, he decided to harm him through some diabolical means. How silly and stupid of him to think that way!

The point of this true-life story is to show that some relationships are just not worth the pain and sacrifice. Some people are the creators of their problems and predicaments.

"Some people are the creators of their problems and predicaments."

Their problems began after they, in the spirit of celebration, decided to organize heavy parties, weddings, or even burial ceremonies in order to excite and please their friends, relatives, neighbors, and communities. After such exposures with people who did not care about their progress, nor were result-oriented, they began to have more enemies than they could manage. Does this then mean that for anyone to become rich he or she must dissociate from ordinary people? Not at all! But billionaires know so well that any enterprise or association that is not result-oriented is bound to create problems for them. Therefore, they choose their associations and the things they engage in wisely.

> *"I don't keep people in my life who are not result-oriented or moving forward."*

One of the main reasons billionaires only keep friends that are result-oriented is to avoid jealousy. I don't keep people in my life who are not result-oriented or moving forward. If I associate with such people, they will become jealous of me and their jealousy will cause me pain and a lot of problems later. To prevent such a scenario, I respectfully decline from engaging in relationships that are not result-oriented and mutually beneficial. The mistake that many poor people make is that they keep people around them who will turn out to be their biggest problems. No matter how kind, gentle, and good-mannered a person may be, if he or she does not have a good vision for the future and concrete goals to back that vision and you keep hanging around such a person, you will soon realize that you don't have definite goals in life.

Avoid Making Excuses

Giving excuses is a luxury that billionaires cannot afford. Rich people do not have time to be complaining and whining about such things as unfavorable weather, terrible political climate, high taxes, inflation, lack of connection, their past loss and failures, and many such things that keep

"To be successful, you must take full responsibility for your actions and stop blaming others for your misfortunes.

people poor. Billionaires operate with the mentality that if something seems unfavorable, then it is their responsibility to fix it. In other words, rich people do not waste time blaming others for their misfortunes or giving excuses why they cannot do certain things. They take full responsibility for their actions.

I cannot afford to relate with people who are always giving excuses—excuses about why they are poor, why they fail, and why they cannot do this or that. Why must I waste my time grumbling and blaming situations for my problems as if doing so is going to provide solutions to them? A common feature among most billionaires is that they are known to be constantly grinding. It doesn't matter the amount of money they have in the bank or the position of power and influence that they have already attained, they are always working hard toward their goals, achieving them, and setting new ones. That is the way to grow and continue to maintain your influence in the world.

> *"I cannot afford to relate with people who are always giving excuses—excuses about why they are poor, why they fail, and why they cannot do this or that."*

To be successful, you must take full responsibility for your actions and stop blaming others for your misfortunes. People who are always playing the "victim mentality" do not make meaningful progress in life. Jack Canfield, the author of the bestselling book, *The Success Principles,* put it better: "If you want to be successful, you have to take 100% responsibility for everything that you experience in your life. This includes the level of your achievements, the results you produce, the quality of your relationships, the state of your health and physical fitness, your income, your debts, your feelings—everything!"

One of the myths people, especially in Nigeria, have about rich people is that they are diabolical. Hence, the idea of rich people "using other people's stars." That is, rich people gain their wealth from diabolical rituals that often involve the shedding of innocent blood or mystically stealing other people's destinies. While it will be inappropriate to totally dismiss such permutations about rich people, the fact is that majority of billionaires gain their wealth legitimately by combining the tenets of hard work and building result-oriented relationships.

Understand The Growth Principle

In you want to cultivate result-oriented relationships, you must understand the principle of growth. The nature of our creation presupposes growth. You are supposed to experience growth in all areas of your life consistently. Frustrations and lack of fulfillment in life usually result from lack of progress. It does not matter the amount of money you have or don't have, anytime you find yourself stagnated and not moving forward, you are bound to feel miserable and unfulfilled. Billionaires understand the principle of growth and are always working hard to make progress in all areas of their lives.

Poor people often refer to rich people as greedy simply because rich people do not seem to get tired of hustling and acquiring more riches. What they fail to realize is that without the sense of progress, rich people are going to be frustrated. Because billionaires understand and utilize the growth principle, they are always making progress, discovering new ventures, and amassing wealth in the process.

> *"Personally, if you are not making progress in life, I can't be your friend."*

Personally, if you are not making progress in life, I can't be your friend. Because if I continue to associate with you, jealousy and unnecessary rivalries will begin to surface. Success can be intimidating. It only takes someone who is making progress in life to appreciate the success of another. The reason why the rich are always friends with the rich is because they understand one another, and they don't feel intimidated by the progress of their friends.

CHAPTER SUMMARY

- Result-oriented people have vision, mission, and goals in life.
- You do not only need to have mutually beneficial relationships, but also result-oriented ones.
- Billionaires know so well that any enterprise or association that is not result-oriented is bound to create problems for them.
- To be successful, you must take full responsibility for your actions and stop blaming others for your misfortunes.
- Because billionaires understand and utilize the growth principle, they are always making progress, discovering new ventures, and amassing wealth in the process.

CHAPTER 3
VISIONARY RELATIONSHIPS

"Vision is the picture of the future that produces passion."

– Bill Hybels

Billionaires are visionary people. Let me reiterate that when I talk about billionaires, I am not referring to corrupt politicians who have stolen people's money or become billionaires without working diligently for what they have. This clarification is important because in Africa many people become rich on the sweat of others due to rampant cases of corruption. Those are not the kinds of people I am talking about. And because of this unfortunate situation of rampant cases of corruption, the average African tends to perceive every rich person as corrupt.

Billionaires are visionary. What is a vision? It is the ability to see beyond the ordinary. In other words, a vision has to do with a projection of future goals and a conscientious determination to achieve them. I particularly like the way Bill Hybels defines vision; he says, "Vision is the picture of the future that produces passion." It is visionary people who change the world. A visionary person is someone who is able to see beyond his present circumstances and be excited and passionate about the future. Billionaires are visionary people, and it is not surprising that their circle of influence tends to comprise of people who are changing the world in different ways.

Your Circle of Influence

In my entire life, I am yet to meet a billionaire who is a gossip. Billionaires only associate, relate and interact with people who have a vision. That is why it is difficult for billionaires to waste time gossiping, whining, or

" A visionary person is someone who is able to see beyond his present circumstances and be excited and passionate about the future."

castigating others. They just don't have time. When they meet with others, they have something important that they want to talk about that will be beneficial to them. They are always thinking about their future goals and do not hesitate to seize every opportunity to talk about their visions and goals.

Since gossip always has to do with what is wrong or bad about another person, it follows that people who waste their time gossiping about others are visionless. If you don't have a specific vision in life, you wouldn't mind talking about others who do. One of the ironies of life is that visionaries create goals and accomplish great feats that visionless people revel in talking about either favorably or unfavorably. In the end, visionaries do not really care what you think about what they achieve in life. They are so preoccupied with many goals that they don't have time to waste listening to or reading comments or gossips about who likes or hates them. The moment they achieve one goal, they quickly move to the next big thing.

Let me share with you one of the secrets of rich and famous people: They dominate social media with their content

"One of the ironies of life is that visionaries create goals and accomplish great feats that visionless people revel in talking about either favorably or unfavorably."

and have a large following on those platforms not necessarily because they spend so much time there. What they do is create content for poor and visionless people who spend hours upon hours consuming them. The moment a rich person posts something on social media, he leaves and finds something important to do. Most of them do not have time to read the comments that people make on their posts because doing so will detract them from their vision. In other words, visionaries create contents for visionless people to spend many hours consuming while the visionaries make money in the process.

> *"Since it is difficult to grow above the five people with whom you spend most of your time, it is incumbent on you to choose wisely people that you allow to be part of that circle. "*

Remember, your circle of influence determines to a great extent where you are headed in life. Who are your five closest friends? Are they visionary or visionless? Since it is difficult to grow above the five people with whom you spend most of your time, it is incumbent on you to choose wisely people that you allow to be part of that circle.

Your Conversation

One of the ways to know whether you are visionary or visionless is to pay attention to the predominant conversations that you have daily. With whom are you spending most of your time? What type of content are you always consuming from books, the television, radio, and social media? Who is influencing you the most? These questions are critical for achieving greatness and becoming wealthy.

The daily conversations of billionaires always revolve around their future goals, projects, and plans. I am yet to meet a billionaire that spends time in conversation about useless things that do not have any direct bearing with his vision and goals. When you see a rich person talking on the phone, he is either talking about some projects or contracts

"The daily conversations of billionaires always revolve around their future goals, projects, and plans."

that need to be accomplished or he is speaking with a mutually beneficial acquaintance who is helping him to achieve some of his goals. But when you see a poor person talking on the phone, he is either complaining about certain happenings in society or spreading rumors and gossips about other people. Why does the billionaire's conversational strategy diverge significantly from that of a poor person? The answer is not far-fetched: It is because the billionaire is visionary while the poor person is not.

Your Expectations of Others

I find it difficult to gossip because I have come to realize that there is no perfect human being on earth. Every one of us has one weakness or the other, no matter how we pretend about it or want to hide it. If this is so, then why should I spend valuable time talking about other people's weaknesses as if I were perfect? How does talking about other people's weaknesses help me to achieve my vision and goals? Talking about others only drains you of your vigor and vitality and

"People will always be people and one of the things about people is that they are not perfect."

deprives you of blessings. Unfortunately, this is what most poor people spend most of their time doing. If you are always expecting people to be perfect, you are delusional and not living in the real world. People will always be people and one of the things about people is that they are not perfect. Even the people you trust the most are likely to disappoint you because that is the nature of our humanity.

One of the biggest frustrations you will face in life is to think that there is somebody that is perfect

> *"Rich people expect competence and excellence, but they never expect the people they are dealing with to be perfect."*

out there or to expect perfection from yourself. In fact, if you are always expecting perfection from others, something is wrong with you. Because what you are trying to do is to play your imperfections in others. In other words, your frustrations are a result of you wishing that you could find perfection in others in the areas of your weaknesses. If those expectations are not met, you feel disappointed and become frustrated in your relationships. Instead of focusing on people's strengths, you look for faults. Such attitude creates a melancholic and pessimistic outlook about life and frustrate your efforts.

If you must go into a relationship with anyone—be it business, romance, vocation, or whatever the nature of the relationship—you should expect that you will be dealing with people who are imperfect and are likely to disappoint you. If you imbibe this attitude, it is going to save you a lot of headaches down the road. This is how billionaires think. Rich people expect competence and excellence, but they never expect the people they are dealing with to be perfect. You must run away from any human being who gives you the impression that he or she is perfect or without weakness. Those are wolves in sheep clothing. You will save yourself a lot of trouble if you develop the courage to detach yourself from such people. Do you know that it is much easier for a rich person to forgive an offense than for a poor person to do so? The reason rich people find it easier to forgive is that they do not enter any relationship expecting perfection. This does not mean that they start relationships without giving them good thought. Remember, as we have seen in the previous chapters, billionaires go after mutually beneficial relationships and result-oriented relationships. Despite this, they are radically open-minded because they know that there are many contingencies in life. They set their goals and expectations high, but they are at the same time flexible to expect disappointments.

"Let your conversation be salted with your vision."

Using your time, energy, and resources to gossip about people's flaws and imperfections only goes to show how unwise you are. If you realize that no human being is perfect, you will do well to focus on people's strengths, values, and how they can be of help to you. Many times, I laugh when I hear husbands complaining about their wives' weaknesses and wishing that their spouses could be like someone out there whom they consider an ideal spouse. And some women also do the same. Such people forget that there is always an advantage to every weakness and a disadvantage to every strength. This is where we miss it—and we miss it big time. For every strength that you see in a person, it is always concomitant with an equivalent weakness. The thing

> "If you realize that no human being is perfect, you will do well to focus on people's strengths, values, and how they can be of help to you."

that you see in another person and appreciate is always a cover for their weaknesses. As the saying goes, "You can't eat your cake and have it."

The energy you use to gossip about others or complain about certain situations can be converted to focus on your vision and achieve great things in life. You must desist from what I call *Social Media Witchcraft* where all you do is monitor other people and have something (mostly negative) to say about them. At the end of the day, what would your effort amount to? Nothing! Let your conversation be salted with your vision.Call your friends and talk to them about your vision. Do you know that by merely talking about your vision you have a thirty-five percent chance of achieving it? The truth is that we are living magnets. What this means in practical terms is that we are constantly attracting into our lives people and

situations that correlate to our dominant thoughts. If you are always thinking negative thoughts toward others, that is what you will get. If so, why don't you convert that passion and energy toward your vision and goals? The more you talk about your vision, the more you will be attracting people into your life who will help you to accomplish it. This is how billionaires operate.

CHAPTER SUMMARY

- Billionaires only associate, relate and interact with people who have a vision.
- A visionary person is someone who can see beyond his present circumstances and be excited and passionate about the future.
- The daily conversations of billionaires always revolve around their future goals, projects, and plans.
- Rich people expect competence and excellence, but they never expect the people they are dealing with to be perfect.
- Let your conversation be salted with your vision.

CHAPTER 4

HONEST RELATIONSHIPS

"Most billionaires have an attitude of picking friends that are not perfect, but honest."

– Dr. Stephen Akintayo

Although billionaires know that no human being is perfect and they never expect perfection from anyone, they are nevertheless careful to cultivate honest relationships. An honest relationship by this standard is one that is free from deceit, duplicity, and dishonesty. Most

"An honest relationship by this standard is one that is free from deceit, duplicity, and dishonesty."

billionaires have an attitude of picking friends that are not perfect, but honest.

Billionaires are radically open-minded when it comes to their dealings with others. This does not mean that they blindly engage in business relationships without caring about where their business partners are coming from. In a billionaire's mind, what is of utmost importance is whether the person in question

"Billionaires don't care what you believe; all they care about is whether you are an honest person or not."

has a track record of honesty and sincerity. Billionaires are always careful not to willfully engage in any business dealing or relationship that will constitute a legal battle to them in the future. This is one of the foundational components that guides and informs rich people's decision-making.

Respect Diversity

Billionaires do not see themselves as social revolutionaries or moral activists. They consider themselves businessmen and businesswomen who are out to exchange values with like-minded people. This is why they are able to relate with people irrespective of their backgrounds. They do not have to believe the same thing, look the same way, talk the same way, or even act the same way with the people with whom they deal. All they are after is honesty in business dealings and transactions and care less about people's backgrounds so long as there is a foundational element of honesty in those dealings. The reason why billionaires adopt this attitude is that they are more concerned about the value that others bring to the table than they are about the moral, religious, ethnic, racial, or geographical background of the person. In other words, billionaires don't care what you believe; all they care about is whether you are an honest person or not.

Why is this important? First, if you pay so much attention to people's backgrounds and judge them based on their diversity, you are likely to miss out on many great opportunities. Second, you cannot succeed as a businessman or businesswoman if you fail to embrace diversity and work with it. The fact is that our diversity is an asset rather than a liability. This is how billionaires think. Third, when people realize that you discriminate against them (either overtly or covertly) because of their background, your business is likely to be jeopardized because that is a serious accusation. Hence, the need to be receptive and embrace diversity and not discriminate against others on that basis.

Unlike rich people, poor people emphasize diversity and often blow it out of proportion and in doing so miss many opportunities that would have come to them. It is poor people who always complain that they cannot deal with certain people because they do not like one or two things about the person's background. But for rich people, what matters most is

> "At the top, relationships are not based on perfection or commonalities; they are based on honesty and trust."

not where you are coming from but your track record of authenticity and honesty. If you prove yourself to be an honest person, rich people will not hesitate to work with you despite your background. At the top, relationships are not based on perfection or commonalities; they are based on honesty and trust.

Strive to be Honest

Since authenticity and honesty are the major things that billionaires pay attention to in their relationship, it is important that if you must reach the top, you must strive to be known as someone who possesses these character traits. Because we live in a world that is characterized by deceit, lies, and all kinds of superficialities, if you are honest you will have an advantage over a lot of people. Your honesty will open a lot of doors for you that you cannot begin to imagine.

One thing that many people always fail to realize is that character speaks volumes. Remember, we are not talking about perfection here. If you prove yourself to be someone that is honest and trustworthy in your dealings with one person, that person will tell another person about you and before you know it you will be encircled by many influential people.

Do you know that even armed robbers and people who engage in certain unethical behaviors prefer to have business dealings with people who are honest? The attitude of honesty alone has the potential to bring you to the limelight because such testimonies spread rapidly. If you do not cultivate the attitude of honesty, even if you cheat your way to the top, your character will eventually catch up with you and bring you down.

Be Radically Open-minded

Some of the people that are going to uplift you will not come from your race, religion, or ethnicity.

"One thing that many people always fail to realize is that character speaks volumes."

They may not believe the same things as you, dress like you, talk like you, or act like you. Nevertheless, you will be shocked to find out that they are your destiny helpers. In order to reach the top of the ladder, therefore, you must be radically open-minded about every relationship that you stumble upon because you can never tell what specific person or events will open up the doors of breakthroughs for you. That is why it is important to cultivate an attitude of honesty so that you don't miss some of the special opportunities that may come your way.

It always baffles me when I hear the way some poor people talk. Most of them are so rigid about the kinds of people that they associate with to the point that they are always quick to dismiss people who do not fit into those categories that they have carved out for themselves. No wonder many poor people continue to remain poor because of such prejudices, biases, and sentiments.

> *"To achieve your goals in life, you must operate based on the principle of trust until you find something concrete that will make you distrust others."*

To achieve your goals in life, you must operate based on the principle of trust until you find something concrete that will make you distrust others. If you are always suspicious and prejudiced toward others, do not be surprised if others act toward you in the same way. This is a basic principle of life: What you give is what you get.

CHAPTER SUMMARY

- Honesty is one of the most important things people look out for apart from competence.
- If you develop a track record of honesty, authenticity and intergrity, soon you will be surrounded by people who appreciate those virtues.
- The billionaire is not after perfection but honesty.
- People's backgrounds hardly matter in the business world; don't let your biases cheat you.

POSITIVE RELATIONSHIPS

"Billionaires only allow into their circles people who have an optimistic life view."

– Dr. Stephen Akintayo

One of the keys to success is the ability to maintain a positive mental attitude. Without a positive mental attitude, it is somewhat impossible to create wealth and maintain it. But what is a positive mental attitude? According to Napoleon Hill, who introduced the concept in his book, *Think and Grow Rich,* which has become one of the best-selling books of all times, a positive mental

> *"Without a positive mental attitude, it is somewhat impossible to create wealth and maintain it."*

attitude deals with the ability to maintain an optimistic disposition about life in general irrespective of what the surrounding circumstances may be.

This is one of the secrets of billionaires. Billionaires are not people who are without challenges or problems, but people who choose to always maintain a positive attitude despite many failures, disappointments, and challenges that they are faced with. To consistently maintain a positive mental attitude, billionaires only allow into their circles people who have an optimistic life view. It is not the delight of rich people to hang around people who are pessimistic, nihilistic, and despondent. They know that such relationships are not going to benefit them in the long run. Hanging around negative people will transfer negative energy and hamper you from achieving your vision and goals. Therefore, billionaires only cultivate positive relationships that are not only mutually beneficial but also inspirational and motivational.

> *"It is not the delight of rich people to hang around people who are pessimistic, nihilistic, and despondent."*

Be an Optimist

Since rich people maintain a positive attitude toward life, it follows that one of the ways you can attract them into your life is to maintain a positive attitude. Rather than joining the bandwagon in complaining about unfavorable circumstances and seeing the world as a dangerous place, you must learn to see the positive side of things even if the situation does not make sense to you now.

You need to understand that rich people are overly sensitive about the kind of energy that the people they relate with emit. When they meet you, it only takes them a few minutes to ascertain the kind of person that you are—whether you have positive or negative energy. And this alone can determine whether they want to do business with you or not. As someone famously said, "Your attitude determines your altitude." If you are the type who always wants to talk about all the negative things that are happening in the world, no serious person will want to relate with you, much less doing business with you.

"Optimism does not mean that you are delusional and fail to see the things that are happening around you for what they really are."

Optimism does not mean that you are delusional and fail to see the things that are happening around you for what they really are. Rather, an optimistic mindset helps you to project your mind beyond your immediate circumstances with hope and confidence that everything will work out for your benefit. As Norman Vincent Peale, the author of the best-selling book,

> *"Learn to exercise some control over your circumstances rather than allowing your circumstances control how you feel and how you act."*

The Power of Positive Thinking, explained it, "You can permit obstacles to control your mind to the point where they are uppermost and thus become the dominating factors in your thought pattern. By learning how to cast them from the mind, by refusing to become mentally subservient to them, and by channeling spiritual power through your thoughts, you can rise above obstacles which ordinarily might defeat you."

Learn to exercise some control over your circumstances rather than allowing your circumstances control how you feel and how you act. It is lugubrious to see how some people live their lives. Because of the lack of discipline to train themselves to have an optimistic mindset, they have allowed themselves to become slaves to their circumstances and the people in their lives so much so that they always feel defeated, incapacitated, and immobilized by the many things that are happening either for them or against them.

Be an Enthusiast

You are probably familiar with the saying: Happiness is a choice. While thinking about this peripherally will not make any logical sense, the reality is that your happiness does not depend on anyone else but you. As Will Smith once said, "Your happiness is your responsibility and your responsibility alone." If you must attract riches into your life, you must be disciplined to be excited about life and the many good things it has to offer. When you wake up in the morning, you need to be excited that you are still alive and that means yet another opportunity to do something worthwhile with your life.

When things go wrong, have a way of seeing the positivity in it. You do yourself a great disservice

"If you must attract riches into your life, you must be disciplined to be excited about life and the many good things it has to offer."

when you allow the things in your life to dictate the way you feel—your state of joy or sadness. The fact is, in life things are bound to go awry and terribly wrong. The problem is not whether things are going to go wrong but how you choose to react to such situations *when* they come.

One of the principles I work with is to only surround myself with optimists and enthusiasts—people who have learned to see the positive in every situation or at the least do not immerse themselves in all the negativities going on in the world. As such, if you are negative, you can't last around me. If you are the kind of person that anytime you see an opportunity you start saying negative things like, "This is not for people like us," or "This is beyond my capability," you and I will find it difficult to understand each other or go far in our relationship. When you see something good and the next thing you are thinking about is, "This is not for people like us," the question I have for you is simple: If it is not for people like you, then what kind of people is it for? It is certainly not for people who have five heads and ten legs. When such thoughts come to mind, always turn them around and ask yourself: If not for me, then who?

Get Rid of Poverty Mentality

You cannot create riches or amass wealth if you are always judging yourself by your current economic condition. You need to realize that your current bank account is not a statement that you are poor. Poverty, in the strict sense, is an attitude of the mind. If you are the type who likes to judge their worth

"You cannot become rich by merely thinking about wealth. Nevertheless, thinking about wealth is the first and foundational stage in wealth creation."

based on their state of insolvency and indebtedness, you will continue to be in that state and never make any meaningful progress in life.

Once wealth is in your mind, it is just a matter of time before it physically manifests. But if what constantly

"You cannot create riches or amass wealth if you are always judging yourself by your current economic condition."

occupies your mind is a poverty mentality, that is what will continue to manifest in your life. You create your reality by your thought patterns. Let me categorically say here that this is not a mumbo-jumbo talk of "Claim it and have it." You cannot become rich by merely thinking about wealth. Nevertheless, thinking about wealth is the first and foundational stage in wealth creation.

I don't care what is in your pocket or bank account right now. If you can substitute your negative, poverty mentality with a positive, wealth mentality, I bet you that you will become rich. This point is important and worth reiterating: The first step to becoming rich is getting rid of a poverty mentality and embracing a wealth mentality. As they say, "Money has ears." Money will be shy to come to you if you are always thinking about poverty—the things that you don't have and your socioeconomic background.

While in the university, I started reading books about positive mental attitudes, the secrets of wealth creation, and the likes. I was poor physically but mentally I considered myself a rich person. Of course, most of my friends did not understand what I was doing. They thought I was going out of my mind. But see where I am today.

When I meet you and decipher that you have a positive mental attitude, that is enough to make me want to be your friend. You may not have money today and nothing in your present circumstances may point to riches, but it does not matter. What matters, amongst other things discussed in prior chapters, is your mental attitude. I don't hesitate to befriend people who defy their present circumstances and believe that they will become rich. Such are the kinds of people that I am always attracted to. But you can't be my friend when your tongue is always negative. Your background is not the reason why your back is on the ground. We all came from a poor background. You need to believe that you too are among rich people. That is the starting point. You may not have it today, but you've got to start seeing yourself that way.

"Your background is not the reason why your back is on the ground."

I am a living testimony that you can turn your life around by cultivating a positive mental attitude. My mother was a junior staff in the civil service. My father's business had collapsed before my birth. I was born in Maiduguri in the Northern part of Nigeria where there was no electricity and running water. I grew up not knowing most of the children's cartoons because though we had a television, we never had electricity. By every standard, I was supposed to end up poor. But as I started reading books, I knew I was going to be wealthy. I started speaking like a rich man. I constantly wore faded jeans, but I kept telling my friends in the university that I was going to be one of the richest people in the world. Most of them could not but laugh at me. Some thought I was arrogant or simly going insane. They would say things like: "The kinds of books he has been reading are making him delusional." But I didn't allow their negativity to affect me. But a few years down the road, my though patterns, mindset and words have led to the manifestation of my present reality.

"Your mental attitude is a key determinant of how far you can go on life's journey."

Everything starts with your mindset. Your mental attitude is a key determinant of how far you can go on life's journey. Billionaires know this secret that is why they only pick friends who are positive in their attitude, words, and behavior. Remember we mentioned earlier that association influences!

Sometimes I cringe when I listen to people talk. Everything they say is wrapped in a poverty mentality. I usually wonder: Why do you think like that? Who decreed you are poor? If you want to be rich, begin with your mind. It is time you do a mental reset.

CHAPTER SUMMARY

- You create your reality by your thought patterns.
- You cannot become rich by merely thinking about wealth. Nevertheless, thinking about wealth is the first and foundational stage in wealth creation.
- You cannot create riches or amass wealth if you are always judging yourself by your current economic condition.
- If you must attract riches into your life, you must be disciplined to be excited about life and the many good things it has to offer.
- Again, association influences; so stay within the circle of positivity—with thought patterns that are forward moving, hopeful and confident that "It'll work out!"

PART TWO

HONOR & FRIENDSHIP CODES

Does honor play a role in mutually beneficial relationships; in all the kinds of relationships outlined in the previous part of this book? Yes.

Billionaires honor one another. They practice the principle of respect and honor to get what they want. They expect same honor, too, from business partners and friends. In other words, honor must be reciprocal. Honor, therefore, is a powerful code that billionaires use to open many doors.

When it comes to friendship, Billionaires befriend other billionaires, not based on tribal, ethnic, racial, religious, or political sentiments. Friendship for them is an opportunity for expanding one's valuable network, opportunities, and business. At the base of their friendships there's honour. Chapter 6 sheds light on this.

CONGENIAL FRIENDSHIP

"A congenial friendship is one of honor and mutual benefits."
– Dr. Stephen Akintayo

There is no doubting the fact that like attracts like. Rich people attract rich people and poor people attract poor people. This is partly the reason the rich continue to get richer and the poor continue to stay poor. But this is not so because rich or poor people love stereotypes. It is because people of like minds and socio-economic class find it much easier to associate with one another. From a sociological perspective, however, similar associations often end up creating classism in society. Such classism may be intentional or inadvertent. Generally, however, social stratification is often caused by economic systems and unequal wealth distribution in society. Such factors such as people's economic wealth, net value, assets, income, wages, investment dividends, and economic power all play a role in stratification in society. Social stratification, in this sense, becomes the major instrument for associations and interactions in society. It is, therefore, not uncommon to see the rich mostly associating with the rich and the poor associating with the poor.

Billionaires love to associate and do business with other billionaires. Their circles of influence revolve around other billionaires. Two major reasons account for this. The first reason is value system. Most billionaires share similar value systems with other billionaires. Therefore, it is easier for them to relate with fellow billionaires because of their shared values. Values such as consistent hard work, unending hunger for success, unrelenting work ethic, prudent spending, insatiable desire to create solutions, constant readiness to take risks, penchant for thinking big, etc. Because values beget actions and actions beget results, billionaires will naturally gravitate towards their fellow billionaires. The second reason is mutual benefits. Note that it is not a one-sided affair. The average billionaire understands the principle and blessedness of giving. They know that giving must always precede receiving. Billionaires love interacting and socializing with other billionaires who have things that can benefit them just as they have something that can be of benefit too. They loathe parasitic associations.

"Billionaires love to associate and do business with other billionaires."

Honor and Friendship

Let's talk about the role of honor in friendship as far as billionaires are concerned. A congenial friendship is one of honor and mutual benefits. We have looked at the fact that billionaires are very mindful of the kind of friendship association they keep, prioritizing mutual benefits over any other thing. It is important to state that billionaires are able to achieve this because they understand the principle of honor. Honor means high respect or great esteem. This means that billionaires hold their fellow billionaires in high esteem. You can only attract what you honor. In fact, it is honor that sustains friendships. Hence, friendship and honor are inseparable. Billionaires understand this principle well and it works in their favor.

I see a lot of people dishonor billionaires in the name of piety. These people glory in self-righteousness and are quick to teach billionaires how to spend their money. You hear things like, "That amount of money could have been used to feed the poor." There was a video of Richard Branson flying into space aboard a rocket he helped fund. You could see the excitement all over him and how much the feat meant to him. On the thread of comments on this video on his LinkedIn handle, you just had to see the tons of people castigating him for investing in such "frivolity" when the money could have been invested in making life easier for poor people. There were a lot of dishonoring words hurled at the billionaire.

There is a heartfelt detest for billionaires by some people because of their wealth, yet these same set of people secretly desire to become wealthy. It doesn't work like that. What you don't honor, you cannot attract into your life. How do you prove that you honor someone? It's by the way you think about them, the way you talk about them, the way you treat them when you are around them, etc. Honor cannot be faked. Billionaires understand the honor code, so they honor their fellow billionaires and this helps them to stay atop in their wealth status.

Don't be a Pawn of the Community Impoverishment Club

Most Africans operate with the philosophy of *community impoverishment*. Community impoverishment is an ideology that says, "If I am not prospering, then I must make sure that I do everything possible to bring down anyone within

> *"Most Africans operate with the philosophy of community impoverishment."*

my circle who appears to be prospering." People who work with this mentality make sure that if one among them appears to be rising on the socio-economic ladder, they connive to impoverish the person by making unnecessary financial requests and placing too many demands on him. As long as that person continues to want to please them, it will just be a matter of time before he loses everything he has accumulated.

Members of the 'Community Impoverishment Club' collectively connive to make the rising stars among them fall. This explains why most Africans who start making money are always hesitant to disclose it to their family members and friends. They understand the intricacies of the African culture and how others may want to impoverish them overnight just because they have started climbing the ladder of success. Until Africans grow above the community impoverishment culture, we are going to remain backward.

> *"Billionaires keep their money close to them. They make sure their money is circulating around them."*

If after making your first million you still surround yourself with poor friends, it is just a matter of time before you lose everything. If you are wise, that is the time to start surrounding yourself with fellow millionaires. And that's how you change your life. By merely associating with millionaires, you gain wisdom on how to multiply your income and increase your social capital which will inevitably multiply your economic worth.

Put a Price Tag on Your Friends

Billionaires keep their money close to them. They make sure their money is circulating around them. They ensure their money is moving within the same circle. The way they achieve this is by carefully and conscientiously choosing their friends. They do not befriend people randomly. What they do is to constantly evaluate each of the people in their social circle based on the value those people add to them. If after an evaluation they consider a particular person not to be of any good value to them, they do not think twice before dissociating with such a person.

If you study the unwritten Jewish business code, it is one of the powerful secrets of the Jews. The code simply says that

"If after making your first million you still surround yourself with poor friends, it is just a matter of time before you lose everything."

no Jew must buy from a non-Jew what a Jewish man sells. If a Jewish man is selling a phone, all the Jews in that community are going to buy their phones from that Jewish man. That way, all their money is retained and keeps circulating among members of their community. The motive of this code is not to promote sectarianism, tribalism, or nepotism. Instead, it is meant to promote business entrepreneurship and prosperity among the community of the Jews who are often few in places like the United States of America.

This is one of the secrets of the American Jews who are among the richest in the world. Most of them are also remarkably successful. It has been discovered that among the top 100 rich people in America, most are either Jews or have Jewish lineage—mother, father, grandparents, great-grandparents, and so forth.

The Jewish Code is the billionaire code. Billionaires patronize each other. It is no longer news that Aliko Dangote is building the largest single chain refinery in the world. The person that is helping supervise the work is his Nigerian billionaire friend, Femi Otedola. Because Otedola has a

"It is much easier for a billionaire to trust another billionaire with a billion dollars than to trust a poor man with such an amount of money."

background in the oil and gas industry and is also a billionaire, it is much easier for Dangote to trust him to handle his billion-dollar project. Not only is Dangote engaging the services of Otedola, but he is also engaging the services of other billionaires. Most of the contracts in the refinery were given to billionaires. The reason for that is not farfetched: It is much easier for a billionaire to trust another billionaire with a billion dollars than to trust a poor man with such an amount of money. A billionaire has the capacity to handle a billion dollars. A poor man does not have such a capacity. It takes a billionaire not to run away with billions of dollars. But if you put a poor person in charge of that kind of money, he may end up becoming confused or decide to run away with the money.

To become a billionaire, you must learn to associate with billionaires. And one thing that billionaires do is that they are always exchanging business ideas and money amongst themselves.
Billionaires multiply their money by associating with other billionaires because those other billionaires have billion-dollar projects they can give them as contracts. The billionaire club is a game of business expansion and all billionaires know this.

One particular January, I hosted a friend, who is a billionaire, in my house. As we were talking, he told me that he had good news to share with me. Prior to that announcement, I was just about to start complaining about how hard the month of January could be. Some people even joke that January has two months in one!. He cut me short by telling me he had just secured two projects, one was worth 4.3 billion naira and the other was worth 3.4 billion naira. He went on to tell me he needed people to help him in handling the various aspects of the projects. The people he needed were to handle billions of naira. Unfortunately for me, I wasn't a billionaire then and so he and I knew that I didn't have the capacity to handle some of those projects. So, I didn't get to play a part in any of the projects. That is typically how billionaires think. And this is the reason money keeps circulating and exchanging hands among them.

CHAPTER SUMMARY

- Rich people attract rich people and poor people attract poor people.
- Billionaires love to associate and do business with other billionaires.
- Billionaires keep their money close to them. They make sure their money is circulating around them.
- The billionaire club is a game of business expansion and all billionaires know thi
- Billionaires hold their fellow billionaires in high esteem. You can only attract what you honor.

PART THREE
CONFIDENCE CODE

Nothing meaningful can be achieved without vision and confidence. Billionaires are always confident about their visions and goals. They do not talk about them in terms of things that *may* happen but as things that *will* happen. Such visualized confidence places them above most people who go about pursuing their dreams without passion and a sense of urgency. This confidence spurs them to learn and quickly adopt better ways of doing things. They work smart! And their successes, in turn, greatly boosts their confidence.

Billionaires understand that smart work is more productive and rewarding than just hard work, so they invest in their minds to boost their confidence and aid their smart work. The world loves and celebrates confident people. Billionaires know that and they use confidence to their advantage through smart work. Chapter 7 explains what smart work is all about.

CHAPTER 7
SMART WORK

"If you want to be a billionaire . . . you must learn to work more with your mind than with your physical strength."
– Dr. Stephen Akintayo

I t was Aliko Dangote who once said he does not understand why young people cannot work until two o'clock in the morning. While he did not mean this as a rule, his point must be taken to heart when it comes to the work ethics of billionaires. Although there are many misconceptions about billionaires among the

"The underlying belief of billionaires is that hard work does not kill, it is wrong work that kills."

general public, the fact is that billionaires prioritize hard work. However, they work smarter than they work hard. The underlying belief of billionaires is that hard work does not kill, it is wrong work that kills.

There is a level you get to where you are excited to work smarter than harder. For instance, billionaires do a lot of their work in their private jet, yacht, Rolls Royce, or Bentley. They are working smarter by combining luxury with work. Sometimes, they work from the comfort of their mansions, while lying on the beach, or enjoying the luxury of five star hotels. Billionaires believe that hard work does not kill; it only refines. But their basic understanding of hard work is working smart. Billionaires spend most of their time observing, thinking, meditating, reading, researching, analyzing, and synthesizing. Many poor people, however, do not have these disciplines.

Billionaires have a habit of working hard but what differentiates them from others is that they work smart.

> "Billionaires spend most of their time observing, thinking, meditating, reading, researching, analyzing, and synthesizing."

Let me demonstrate the difference between hard work and smart work with something practical. Think about the various people that work on a construction site. There, you will find a laborer, foreman, engineer, supervisor, and contractor. Now, the laborer works physically hard than all the rest, but he earns the least amount. The foreman works less physically hard than the laborer but earns more than the laborer. The engineer works less physically hard than the foreman, but he earns more than the foreman. The supervisor works less physically hard than the engineer, but he earns more than him. And the same goes for the contractor who does little or no physical work at all but earns more than what the supervisor and all the other workers receive. Why is this so? Is it unfair that the ones who physically work hard toward the success of the project receive the least pay? To answer this question, one must understand that working smart is a mind game. While the laborer uses his physical strength to earn a living through hard work and daily toiling and may remain poor, the supervisor uses his mind to generate great wealth.

Using our analogy of a construction site, the foreman is paid more than the laborer not because the foreman works physically harder than him, but because he applies his mental faculties to his work more than the laborer. All that the laborer is concerned about is using his physical strength to accomplish certain tasks. The foreman earns more than the laborer because he does more mental work than the laborer. So goes the differentiation up the ladder. The less physical work you do and apply mental work, the higher your pay. Conversely, the more physical work you do at the expense of mental work, the lower your pay in the market space. This is the secret to billionaire work habits. But because of the misunderstanding of this basic and yet difficult concept, many poor people end up getting mad and resentful toward billionaires because they see them as people who do not work hard but have all the money in the world while those who work hard seem to suffer perpetually. This has always been the poor man's dilemma from one generation to another.

Think

Napoleon Hill, in his all-time bestselling books, *Think and Grow Rich,* said, "Truly, 'thoughts are things,' and powerful things at that, when they are mixed with definiteness of purpose, persistence, and a burning desire for their translation into riches, or other material objects." The power of thinking for generating wealth cannot be overemphasized. Becoming wealthy is essentially a mental game because wealth originates with our thoughts. It is a truism that your thoughts become your reality.

Billionaires understand the importance of thought in generating wealth and make it the center of their daily activities. In other words, thinking occupies most of the billionaire's daily life. In short, thinking is the centerpiece that controls

"Becoming wealthy is essentially a mental game because wealth originates with our thoughts. It is a truism that your thoughts become your reality."

and directs the habits of billionaires. Thus, understanding the importance of thinking for success in life and business, enjoy working hard but prefer to work smarter. They know that if they train themselves to think critically, objectively, and positively, there is no problem that comes up in their life or business that will be insurmountable. I, for instance, seldom exert physical strength or energy for the purpose of accomplishing my personal and business goals. Instead, I do a lot of mental work. That is what it means to work smart.

Billionaires work smart. They think about working smart than they do about working hard. As such, they do a lot of mental work. They are always thinking about how to improve their businesses, contacts, relationships, human and material resources. They are always thinking about ways to make their work more efficient and effective. They are always thinking about how to expand their businesses and scale them. They are always thinking about the next big thing either in their life or business. They are always thinking about bigger and more ambitious projects.

If you want to be a billionaire, you must work hard but make sure your hard work is smart work. You must learn to work more with your mind than with your physical strength. One of the ways to engage in objective thinking is to practice meditation. Billionaires practice meditation of different sorts. Some make a habit of sitting in a secluded and serene place at a particular time to meditate. Some prefer to interact with nature while they meditate. Others prefer to just sit quietly where there are less distractions. And others practice yoga. It all depends on personal preferences. Most billionaires practice meditation (or mental work) for a minimum of one hour daily. But meditation is not so much about the length of the practice as it is about its effectiveness.

Do you plan to create wealth? If you do, then you must learn to cultivate a daily routine of thinking and meditation. You must imbibe the habit of creative imagination. It was Albert Einstein who said, "Imagination is everything. It is the preview to life's coming attraction." A habit of daily thinking and meditation would likely lead to creative imagination

> *"Do you plan to create wealth? If you do, then you must learn to cultivate a daily routine of thinking and meditation. You must imbibe the habit of creative imagination."*

whereby you begin to manifest what your thoughts create. How many times in a week do you sit down to meditate? Remember, meditation is also known as mental regurgitation.

Analyze

Most billionaires are good observers. They try to understand contemporary trends and cultures so that they will stay well-informed. This is because they know that whatever is happening in the socio-economic and political domains will invariably affect their businesses whether for good or for bad. Therefore, they always try to stay atop societal happenings so that they can make informed and wise decisions about their businesses. Observation is a key component that ennobles imaginative thinking.

But while billionaires love imaginative thinking, they do not stop there. Through observation and creative imagination, they learn to analyze and synthesize their thoughts to produce great results. Hence, they pay a great deal of attention to detail as they observe, think, and imagine. When they have a difficult project or problem at hand, billionaires love to engage in critical analysis of the issue. They examine it from every angle, seeking the right solution. They scrutinize the project or situation and try to see how best to handle it. They are always thinking and asking critical questions. How can I run this business better? How can we make the products and services in our company more efficient and profitable? Are there better ways to go about executing this project? Their thinking may become cyclical, but it is for a purpose. They think about such questions over and over until they arrive at a better solution.

One may assume that such critical thinking is a boring and nonsensical process, but it is the secret of billionaires. One of my billionaire mentors, for instance, does not sleep until three o'clock in the morning every day. Between 12 midnight and three o'clock in the morning, he is often reading, thinking, and writing. In the quietude of the night, he takes his time to think, meditate, analyze, and put down his thoughts in writing. This has been one of his powerful secrets.

> *"When they have a difficult project or problem at hand, billionaires love to engage in critical analysis of the issue."*

Here is a thought-provoking question: What percentage of their time do poor people spend thinking, meditating, and analyzing their lives and businesses? Most poor people find analytical thinking and creative imagination boring and a waste of time. They are always in a rush to decide what to do, how to spend their money, people to call on the phone, and other such mediocre decisions that end up disorganizing their time, energy, and resources. Billionaires hardly take rash decisions. They have trained themselves, through consistently

> *"Billionaires hardly take rash decisions. They have trained themselves, through consistently applied self-discipline, to be critical and logical thinkers."*

applied self-discipline, to be critical and logical thinkers. That is why they are not mediocre.

To demonstrate how seriously they prioritize critical thinking, most billionaires have a Think Tank—a group of experts saddled with the responsibility of analyzing and synthesizing problems to find logical answers and solutions. Billionaires are never shy or afraid to ask questions or seek clarity for what they do not understand. But most poor people are arrogant and proud, often feeling that by asking questions people are going to look down on them. This way, they die in their ignorance.

Read

There is no doubting the fact that most billionaires are avid and voracious readers. Reading is part of their daily routine. Warren Buffett, for instance, is said to spend eighty percent of his day reading. Some resources show that he reads an average of five hundred pages every day. Bill Gates is said to read at the speed of 150 pages per hour, totaling fifteen books per week. Mark Cuban, an American billionaire entrepreneur and investor, is said to read for an average of three hours per day. And when you study other billionaires like Oprah Winfrey, Mark Zuckerberg, Elon Musk, Jeff Bezos, and the likes, the common denominator among them is the discipline of spending a meaningful time for daily reading.

This is one of the major secrets of billionaires. They read to stay ahead of the competition and make informed decisions. Because they don't want to appear ignorant about any subject, they try to read widely. In other words, they do not limit their readings to the areas of their specialization. Their readings are focused and all-encompassing.

An average billionaire reads at least a book or two in a week. But most poor people hardly read one book in a year. They see reading as a waste of time. They would prefer to spend hours on social media watching comedies and paying attention to useless gossips—habits that only take from them. If you want to measure whether you are well-positioned to create wealth, here is a simple test for you: How many books (and on what topics) have you read in the past few months? Your honest response to this question should point you to where you currently are on the ladder of wealth creation.

"There is no doubting the fact that most billionaires are avid and voracious readers. Reading is part of their daily routine."

CHAPTER SUMMARY

- Billionaires prioritize hard work. However, they work smarter than they work hard.
- Billionaires spend most of their time observing, thinking, meditating, reading, researching, analyzing, and synthesizing.
- Becoming wealthy is essentially a mental game because wealth originates with our thoughts.
- When they have a difficult project or problem at hand, billionaires love to engage in critical analysis of the issue.
- Billionaires hardly take rash decisions. They have trained themselves, through consistently applied self-discipline, to be critical and logical thinkers.

PART FOUR

PURPOSE CODE

If there is a group of people who know the importance of pursuing purpose, billionaires are at the fore. Everything about them is often geared toward a specific purpose. In other words, they know why they are here and have a clear vision about where they are going. Due to this, they are not easily distracted. They do not take on a blur trail and distinctly have their intentions mapped in their closest views.

In all of these, their imperfection as humans could mean that they might be faced head-on with failure at one time or another. If this happens, their response is the only thing that makes the difference. Having previously discussed the impotance of positive relationships, how do billionaires handle failures, disappointments, and discouragements? Are there times that billionaires may decide to abandon the pursuit of a specific purpose when it does not seem to be working? How often do they change direction in the pursuit of their purpose? How about we walk a few steps closer to getting answers to these "Hows" in Chapter 8?

FOCUSED ENERGY

"Focused energy implies the ability to concentrate your thoughts and efforts on what you want to see manifest."

– Dr. Stephen Akintayo

E nergy is everything. Without it, all things will likely crumble. Nothing worthwhile can be achieved without energy. You need constant energy to keep up with the daily demands of life and business. But not any kind of energy; you need focused energy. Billionaires work and thrive on focused and sustained energy. They are filled with enthusiasm and zest about what they do. That—enthusiasm and zeal—are the very starting point of anything that will last through challenges.

There is a clear connection between financial success and thought energy. You cannot build wealth if you are constantly focusing your energy on the wrong things. Your productivity in life is largely determined by your thought energy. What you concentrate on is where your energy goes. Billionaires understand the importance of focused energy. Focused energy implies the ability to concentrate your thoughts and efforts on what you want to see manifest. Doing this requires discipline.

> *"Billionaires gain energy from mockery."*

As you begin to ascend the ladder of success, many people will feel threatened by your accomplishments and may want to do things to distract you. They will castigate, disparage, and try to belittle you. If you pay attention to their negative energy, you will soon lose focus. To avoid such negative distractions, you must train your mind to remain focused on your goals and the things you set out to do.

> *"Billionaires work and thrive on focused and sustained energy. They are filled with enthusiasm and zest about what they do."*

Don't Take the Bait

Billionaires gain energy from mockery. When they start in a small and humble way, because people may not see what they are seeing, they are likely to mock and laugh at them. They may call them names, and it is not uncommon for some people to try to do everything to stop them. They may tell them that they have lost their minds to think that they can achieve what they set out to do. But instead of becoming discouraged by such wet blankets, the visionaries who often turn out to become billionaires are often energized by such discouragements and disapprovals. The more people try to criticize and discourage them from pursuing their vision, the more they become energized to focus on it to prove them wrong.

Billionaires are visionaries. They understand that in life, people don't pay attention to those who do what is expected of them. But the moment one decides to be a nonconformist—to break the barrier of doing what is quotidian—suddenly everyone begins to pay attention and feels uncomfortable by such initiatives. Because many people go through life without having the courage to pursue their dreams and ambitions, they easily feel threatened and become envious of those who have the effrontery to go after their dreams. Paulo Coelho described such attitude better in his famous book, *The Alchemist,* when he said, "If someone isn't what others want them to be, the others become angry. Everyone seems to have a clear idea of how other people should lead their lives, but none about his or her own."

Billionaires understand this basic human psychology and they are never discouraged by other people's mocking and disdaining attitudes. They never allow themselves to be distracted or sidetracked by people whose aim is to bring them down. Once they fix their gaze on a goal, billionaires direct their energy there and work relentlessly to achieve it. This does not mean that they are oblivious to the reality of challenges and difficulties that are on the path to greatness. They know about such challenges and are always ready to face them headlong. One thing they don't do is to take the bit that negative onlookers throw at them on their journey to the top.

Stay Constantly Focused

Most billionaires were at one point or the other mocked by their friends, colleagues, and even family members for being

"It is one thing to have a dream, but it is another thing to pursue it to its logical conclusion. Having a dream is easy. Anyone can have grandiose dreams."

too ambitious or building a castle in the air. Instead of getting discouraged by such remarks and mockeries, they were energized by them. As people kept throwing baits at them that would have swerved their focus from their vision, they refused to take it. They remained relentless, persistent, and consistent until they achieved their goals to the amazement of those who thought that they could not do that which they set out to do.

It is one thing to have a dream, but it is another thing to pursue it to its logical conclusion. Having a dream is easy. Anyone can have grandiose dreams. The problem is having the courage to step out and stay long enough in pursuit of the dream to bring it to fruition. Many people who live mediocre lives are not people without dreams. They probably have more dreams than billionaires. Unfortunately, billions of such people live and die with their dreams without even trying because they are afraid of what others might think of them; afraid they might fail—again.

> *"Once they fix their gaze on a goal, billionaires direct their energy there and work relentlessly to achieve it."*

Billionaires, however, will rather go after their dreams and fail than not try at all. They understand Paulo Coelho's observation that "It's the possibility of having a dream come true that makes life interesting." Therefore, they are never afraid to try. And when they set out after their dreams, they focus and direct all their energy toward it until it materializes.

Be a 'No-Matter-What' Person

To have focused and sustained energy, you must train yourself to be a no-matter-what person. A no-matter-what person is someone who sets out to do something with definiteness of purpose and is willing to do everything it takes to bring it to pass, despite foreseeable difficulties and obstacles. All it takes to be a no-matter-what person is to have an unshakable will.

One of the characteristics of our humanity is that when we are determined to do something and totally commit ourselves to it, we can surmount every challenge that may come before us and our goals.

> *"To have focused and sustained energy, you must train yourself to be a no-matter-what person."*

Benjamin Disraeli, one of the famous Prime Ministers of the United Kingdom, once said, "Nothing can withstand the power of the human will if it is willing to stake its very existence to the extent of its purpose." That is quite true about the nature of our humanity.

Becoming a no-matter-what person helps you to see life differently. It changes your perspectives about people's opinions about you, especially those which are meant to discourage you from attaining your goals. A no-matter-what person is not unnecessarily concerned or bothered about the negative opinions of others. I have a maxim that 'people must mock you for God to make you.' One of the tests of success is overcoming the need to please people. If you overcome the fear of what other people think about you, you are on your way to the top.

> *"I have a maxim that 'people must mock you for God to make you."*

The fear of what others think is what keeps many people down and hinders them from pursuing purpose. Rather than being unnecessarily concerned about what others think, you must learn to refocus that energy toward thinking about your life legacies. A clear life vision is a necessary antidote for overcoming the fear of other people.

Billionaires understand that mockery and derision by others are unavoidable. Therefore, they do not waste their energy ruminating about what other people think or say about them.

> *"It will be something of a miracle for anyone to fulfill destiny without passing through the waters of mockery. Mockery is to vision what fire is to gold. You cannot have one without the other."*

They know that in life, no matter what you do, people are going to talk about you unfavorably. You can never please everyone. I have never seen any billionaire that does not have his or her equal share of mockery. When Aliko Dangote started his company, he was mocked and derided. When Jack Ma started his company, he was not only misunderstood but he was also mocked. And the list can go on. Every billionaire was at one point or the other misunderstood and mocked by others. Imagine if they had given up because of mockery. We probably would not have Microsoft, Apple computers and iPhones, digital marketing like Amazon, and a host of other great innovations of the modern era.

People will mock you once you start going after a worthwhile goal. They must mock you for God to make you. You must learn to enjoy the mockery and be energized by it. If people do not see any reason to mock you, it is a sign that you are not fulfilling destiny. If people do not mock

"A clear life vision is a necessary antidote for overcoming the fear of other people."

you, you are probably not maximizing destiny and fulfilling your potential. It will be something of a miracle for anyone to fulfill destiny without passing through the waters of mockery. Mockery is to vision what fire is to gold. You cannot have one without the other.

Because every great destiny needs to start small, it is understandable that shortsighted people are going to deride, disparage, and disdain visionaries. Hence, it is important to never despise the days of your little beginnings. When I started my company, many people said I was mentally deranged. Some simply said I was acting foolishly. Some who couldn't stand my guts said all kinds of unfounded things to discourage my efforts. But I never allowed myself to be distracted by such things. I have remained focused on my vision and never looked back. Such is the attitude of billionaires. They have focused energy that is never impeded by the surrounding circumstances.

CHAPTER SUMMARY

- Focused energy, the persistence to keep your eyes on your goal and work towards it, will see you through the daily demands of life and business.
- Your productivity in life is largely determined by your thought energy. What you concentrate on is where your energy goes.
- It is one thing to have a dream, but it is another thing to pursue it to its logical conclusion.
- To have focused and sustained energy, you must train yourself to be a no-matter-what person.
- It will be something of a miracle for anyone to fulfill destiny without passing through the waters of mockery. Mockery is to vision what fire is to gold. Instead of getting beat down by it, be spurred on!

PART FIVE

PHILOSOPHY CODE

All humans have motivations for doing what they do. The motivations for our actions constitute our philosophy of life. Philosophy is a concept personal to every individual because we think and reason from different perspectives. Hence, there is no generally acceptable philosophy. Some of our life philosophies may be known to us and others may not be so known, but we are nevertheless the sum of those philosophies, our behaviors being guided by them.

Our philosophies give us the daily impetus to pursue our goals, persevere and keep going when the journey gets tough. The philosophy of balance, importantly, is crucial and necessary for success. We see more of it in Chapter 9.

BALANCED LIFE

"Billionaires are ready to endure today's pain for the sake of tomorrow's pleasure . . . that's balance."
– Dr. Stephen Akintayo

Humans naturally gravitate toward extremes. This is why there seem to be many dualities and polarities in life. We talk about hot or cold, rich or poor, bitter or sweet, happy or sad, pain or pleasure, good or evil, war or peace, and many of such things. By thinking of life in terms of polarities, we create stereotypes and limit the human experience to either one thing or another.

> *"By thinking of life in terms of polarities, we create stereotypes and limit the human experience to either one thing or another."*

Regrettably, many people bring such ideas to business. They tend to think of business as something that can either go well or bad, something that is either bitter or sweet, or something that brings constant success or failure. But the reality is that business, and ultimately life, cannot be so categorized. It is a constant mixture of bitter and sweet experiences, successes and failures, pleasure and pain.

> *"Billionaires avoid the common stereotypes that most people have about business. They do not see business as either sweet or bitter; instead, they approach it as a sweet-bitter experience."*

Billionaires avoid the common stereotypes that most people have about business. They do not see business as either sweet or bitter; instead, they approach it as a sweet-bitter experience. This is why they can endure pain and failures at one time, and enjoy pleasure and success at the other. They understand that business is all about balance. Therefore, they are not afraid to fail to try, nor do they avoid taking responsibility for their failures.

Take Some Pain

It is impossible to meet any billionaire who is not familiar with pain. While many people only know about the successes of billionaires, no one seems to take note of the many pains, heartbreaks, failures, and predicaments that billionaires have endured over the years to get to where they are. Most people think of billionaires as people who have always succeeded. But nothing could be further from the truth.

Billionaires, just like most people, are acquainted with pain. They know what it means to try and fail. They know what it means to be disappointed. They know what it means to be betrayed, castigated, blackmailed, derided, disparaged, and chided. They know what it means to be rejected, scorned, and despised. But through it all, they have learned to endure their pain, suffering, and failures to get to where they want to be.

Every good thing that will be successful must be tested. As such, billionaires understand that for them to succeed, they must be ready to remain resolute and dogged during moments of pain and failure. They have a good grasp of what Napoleon Hill famously observed that "all who succeed in life get off to a bad start, and pass through many heartbreaking struggles before they 'arrive.' The turning point in the lives of those who succeed usually comes at the moment of some crisis, through which they are introduced to their 'other selves.'" Another of Hill's statements that has been popularized in this regard is this: "Every adversity, every failure, every heartache carries with it the seed of an equal or greater benefit."

It seems as if before life gives you something good, it must test you through trials and difficulties to validate the tenacity of your desire. Billionaires understand this principle about life that they are never hasty to cower to any challenges or difficulties. They are not only familiar with pain, but they also use it to their own advantage.

> *"It seems as if before life gives you something good, it must test you through trials and difficulties to validate the tenacity of your desire."*

However, many poor people do not have this understanding of pain. They think of pain in terms of failure and as a sign that a particular path is not worth the effort. When life tests them, they fail because their socio-economic conditions have made them develop negative attitudes toward pain. They see pain as something negative which does not have the potential of generating something good in the future.

But billionaires know how to balance pain and pleasure, the bitter and the sweet. They are ready to take the pain because they know it is a momentary experience that has the potential of paving the way for great success. But one of the

> *"Billionaires are ready to endure today's pain for the sake of tomorrow's pleasure."*

things I realize with a lot of poor people is that they do everything possible to try to avoid pain, not knowing that on your way to greatness there are just certain kinds of pain and suffering that are inevitable. The most painful thing about poor people's avoidance of pain is that they always end up living in consistent pain. If pain avoidance is not a guarantee of not having pain, then why not just face it off with hope and optimism that it would lead to greater or equivalent advantage? Billionaires are ready to endure today's pain for the sake of tomorrow's pleasure.

I have experienced and endured a great deal of pain to be where I am today. Years ago when I started, I remember trekking long distances while sweating and crying just to make ends meet. On one particular occasion when I started my digital marketing, I had to walk on foot for a long distance in Lagos State, Nigeria, pasting the advertisement posters of my business. Because I didn't have the capital to pay for radio and television advertisements, I had to take the pain to use what was available and affordable through a painful process. I started pasting those posters at ten o'clock in the morning and by the time I was done, it was

". I kept working resiliently and persistently against all odds because I knew where I was going. I understood the spiritual principle that weeping may endure for a night but rejoicing comes in the morning."

midnight. I won't forget once coming down from a bus with tears rolling down my cheeks because of the suffering and pain that I

had to go through. I thought to myself: How can a university graduate like me suffer this much? But my pain did not deter me. I kept working resiliently and persistently against all odds because I knew where I was going. I understood the spiritual principle that weeping may endure for a night but rejoicing comes in the morning. So, I worked hard and defied all the odds that were on my way.

During the days of my painful struggles, there was a particular instance when tears began to roll down my eyes, it was as if I heard someone ask me, "Why are you crying? A day is coming that you will tell people about this particular ordeal and they will find it difficult to believe you because of the level of success that you would have attained. Some might even call you a liar." Today, when people meet me, they find it difficult to associate my present level of success with those days of humble beginnings. They just cannot reconcile how someone coming from my kind of background could achieve the kind of success that I have already achieved in the realms of entrepreneurship and business. I had to endure great pain to get to where I am today. My story has changed. I now have businesses outside my native country that are thriving. But I first had to suffer and endure pain, betrayal, lack, scorn, blackmails, and disappointments.

Some people criticize me for flaunting my success. They do so because they do not understand where I am coming from. While I do not purposely set out to flaunt my success in a braggadocious manner, I cannot hide my success because my failures were obvious and glaring to everyone. People who saw me suffer and go through all kinds of pain should also see my success to better understand my story.

Billionaires know that pain is a prelude to pleasure and breakthroughs are often preceded by barriers. Therefore, they often endure today's pain because they know that it would not last forever. They are willing to balance between painful and pleasurable experiences without taking any of those experiences for granted. But many people think that life is supposed to be pleasurable always; and so, they unsuccessfully try to escape every kind of pain. Some are on the other extreme, believing life ought to be hard, thus they disbelieve and fight off goodness.

> *"Billionaires know that pain is a prelude to pleasure and breakthroughs are often preceded by barriers."*

If you want to be a billionaire, you must be willing to emulate the work habits of billionaires. One of such habits is to learn to embrace momentary pain. Remember, billionaires are willing to take pain as a pathway to pleasure. They are willing to experience both the sweet and bitter aspects of life because they know that only by doing so would they have a balanced life. They don't embrace the sweet experience and reject the bitter ones. For them, sweet and bitter is the full package. They know that the sweet-bitter experience is what life is all about. Therefore, they do not shy or run away from facing it. They have learned to blend opposite experiences to gain some balance.

Through experience, I know that whenever I am going through a tough and painful time, something good is just around the corner. So, I get excited. Rather than becoming discouraged because of painful experiences, I am always energized by them. Conversely, anytime life seems smooth and pleasurable, I begin to prepare for bad times because I know that something bad may just be about to strike. Someone reading this may think that this is a

"When billionaires are having a good time of success in their business, that is often the time they start preparing for eventualities and contingencies."

rather fatalistic way to approach life, but I bet you that science has proven over and again that this is the operational principle at work in the universe. When billionaires are having a good time of success in their business, that is often the time they start preparing for eventualities and contingencies. They do not wait until disaster, catastrophe, or adversity strikes before they start running helter-skelter looking for a solution. They plan for such things in advance.

Practice Delayed Gratification

Another concept that characterizes billionaires' work ethics is the practice of delayed gratification. Delayed gratification deals with the act of resisting an impulse to succumb immediately to available pleasures that promise an immediate reward to obtain a more beneficial and valued reward sometime in the future. Delayed gratification deals with personal discipline toward self-actualization that is rooted in self-control.

Billionaires operate by the principle of delayed gratification. They understand that life's enticements and entrapments are innumerable, always appealing to our gullible and susceptible nature. But they also know that willfully giving in to such appeals leads to poor financial, personal, and business decisions that can be destructive. Therefore, they have trained themselves to practice delayed gratification to achieve their life and business goals.

To practice delayed gratification, one must be willing to make huge and painful sacrifices. Accordingly, billionaires sacrifice their time, energy, and resources to get better rewards in some future time. They understand that nothing comes to us freely or on a platter of gold. In consequence, they make huge sacrifices by postponing immediate gratification since such sacrifices are likely to bring them unimaginable rewards sooner or later. If there is a serious business to attend to, a billionaire can decide to sleep in his office for three months, forsaking the comforts of his mansion and cozy bed. As I write this, I have been away from my family in Nigeria for three months. My wife and kids only came to see me last month in Dubai for just a few days and went back to Nigeria. I did not see my family for two months consecutively because I was working on a project. For any family man, that is a huge sacrifice to make. Such is the kind of sacrifice that billionaires always have to make if they must achieve their business goals. They are always willing to make tough sacrifices for tomorrow.

> *"To practice delayed gratification, one must be willing to make huge and painful sacrifices."*

But many poor people are not willing to suspend immediate gratification for a better tomorrow. I remember once meeting an old friend who was a banker. He was always complaining about the demands of his work and how the bank was using him, insisting that he could not wait to leave the job.

He shared with me that he wanted to start his own company. At first, I cautioned and counseled him about his seemingly rash decision, pointing him to the fact that starting a business was not an easy thing to do. But he would not listen to my wise counsel. He stood by his decision and in no time, he resigned from his position. Afterward, I gave him some business blueprint that I thought would be helpful to him in his new adventure.

One of the things I specifically advised him to do was to employ a personal assistant. But I met him six months later and gently inquired: "Have you employed a personal assistant yet?" In his response, he narrated to me how difficult it was to find a college graduate that was willing to receive low wages. What most of the graduates who applied for the position were asking for was a salary of forty thousand naira a month, but my friend thought it was outrageous; he wanted to pay twenty-five thousand naira for a start. But guess how much his monthly salary was in the bank when he resigned? Five hundred thousand naira a month. After listening to him narrate his perceived ordeal, I looked at him and confronted him gently but frankly, thus: "You mean that you are unwilling to pay a university graduate like you a meager amount of forty-thousand-naira salary whereas you resigned from a job that paid you five hundred thousand naira and kept complaining that the bank was using you?" The long story short is that his situation is pathetic today. He couldn't succeed in his new startup because he had not learned the principle of delayed gratification.

Until you are willing to sacrifice, you will not succeed in business. We often wish that people would sacrifice for us, but we are not willing to do it for other people. Many employees hate their employers and are dissatisfied with their work because they don't want to sacrifice for today and reap the benefits tomorrow. When such people decide to resign their positions, it is not uncommon to see them mistreat their employees because they have not learned the principle of sacrifice. It takes sacrifice to grow any business. It takes sacrifice to build wealth. It takes time, energy, and resources to be wealthy. You cannot reap where you did not sow.

> *"It takes sacrifice to grow any business. It takes sacrifice to build wealth. It takes time, energy, and resources to be wealthy. You cannot reap where you did not sow."*

I have an older brother who makes huge sacrifices to achieve his business goals. No wonder he is highly successful. A gentle fellow, he sometimes travels and stays for five months in some thick forests because the nature of his business demands that. He is willing to take the pain to keep his business thriving and flourishing. But many unsuccessful people are not willing to make such sacrifices. They might say things like, "I can't afford to leave my family that long," "I can't spend extra two hours at work," "I can't sacrifice my pleasure for the sake of gaining

something better," "I am content with what I have." It is not a surprise that such people end up living in perpetual poverty.

CHAPTER SUMMARY

- By thinking of life in terms of polarities, we create stereotypes and limit the human experience to either one thing or another.
- Billionaires are ready to endure today's pain for the sake of tomorrow's pleasure . . . that's balance.
- Billionaires know that pain is a prelude to pleasure and breakthroughs are often preceded by barriers.
- To practice delayed gratification, one must be willing to make huge sacrifices.
- It takes sacrifice to build wealth. It takes time, energy, and resources to be wealthy. You cannot reap where you did not sow.

PART SIX

ROUTINE CODE

No one has ever achieved anything great without developing and following a routine. Billionaires know the importance of routines and they capitalize on them to achieve great results. Therefore, they put systems in place to help them stick to certain routines long enough for maximum effectiveness and productivity. The Routine Code leverages many studies that have been carried out on the importance of routines for success and achievement and contextualizes those findings with practical examples about billionaires and their lifestyles.

The importance of the Routine Code is laid out in the next two chapters. Chapter 10 examines the important concept of *Moderate Lifestyle,*which shows that prudent financial management is the billionaire's routine. Their expenditure stands commensurate with their income. Chapter 11 examines investment in real and *Consistent Ventures.* It points to the fact that failure to scrutinize and ascertain the authenticity and consistency of investment opportunities is a catastrophic mistake. Thus, due care is another routine of the billionaire.

CHAPTER 10

MODERATE LIFESTYLE

"Moderation . . . is not so much about how much one spends as it is about how much one spends in proportion to his income."

– Dr. Stephen Akintayo

Many people assume that billionaires are extravagant—always buying expensive cars, clothes, and toys. They fail to realize that billionaires are prudent in the way they manage their resources. In fact, such prudence is their "normal"; their day-in, day-out routine. Of course, while billionaires can afford to buy certain things that may seem extravagant to the poor, the reality is that their spending habits are always commensurate with their income. In other words, billionaires are prudent and sagacious in their spending. They do not buy things that they do not need; neither do they spend money just for the sake of spending. Because they plan and budget their expenses, billionaires imbibe the principle of moderation as part of their spending habits.

But most poor people do the complete opposite. They live above their income. In doing so, they incur a lot of debt that takes them many years to repay. Because they have allowed themselves to be entangled by debt through living

> "When your expenses outweigh your income, you are living above your means."

above their means, they find it difficult to become financially independent. A billionaire may purchase a car that is worth two hundred thousand dollars. While this may seem outrageous to many poor people, it may not necessarily be outrageous spending to the billionaire. But if someone who earns a hundred thousand dollars annually decides to buy a car of fifty thousand dollars—*that* could be considered an outrageous and unwise expense. Moderation, therefore, is not so much about how much one spends as it is about how much one spends in proportion to his income.

Cut Your Coat

The adage, "Cut your coat according to your size," is relevant to the principle of moderation. The principle of financial moderation implies that your expenses must be a true

> *"Because they plan and budget their expenses, billionaires imbibe the principle of moderation as part of their spending habits."*

reflection of your financial capability. When your expenses outweigh your income, you are living above your means. It follows that a person who is living above his means has not learned the principle of prudent moderation in financial management.

If you desire to build lasting wealth, you must learn the principle of prudent moderation. It should become a regular thing for you. A routine. One way to do that is to learn to cut your coat according to your size. By implication, you must avoid making purchases and spending money that can jeopardize your income. Before you spend money, always ask yourself the following questions: Do I really need to do this? Is this money I am about to spend a true reflection of my income? Does this expense correspond to my financial status or is it simply an imitation of someone or something?

Billionaires cut their coats according to their size. They do not spend money frivolously just because they have plenty of it. They carefully and judiciously weigh their spending habits based on their need and financial capabilities. Do not buy a Ferrari just because celebrities, and famous people seem to be flaunting it around. The questions to ask are: Why do I need a Ferrari? Am I financially capable to buy and maintain a Ferrari? Of what significance is buying a Ferrari at this point to me? This is how billionaires think.

Don't Compare

One of the problems of contemporary societies, which has been heightened and promulgated by social media, is the urge to compare ourselves with others. We see our friends, peers, neighbors, colleagues, business partners, and even people we do not know, posting pictures of their luxurious lifestyles and "happiness levels" on social media, and we immediately wish we could be like them. Hardly does it occur to us that most of what is usually promoted and showcased on social media is fake—it is not a reflection of reality.

Many people who pay attention to such propaganda on social media often find themselves ensnared by envy, rivalry, and unnecessary competition. They see their friends do something on social media and the next thing they want to do is to copy them and, if possible, outdo them. Such childish behaviors have led many poor people into unending traps. Billionaires do not live their lives that way. They are always busy pursuing a purpose that they hardly have time to track down what their peers are doing, talk more about competing, or trying to outdo them.

"In the realm of financial management, to be wise means to understand the operational principles of wealth creation and maintenance."

Suffice it to say that comparison is a vain venture. While it is in human nature to compete, what Herbert Spencer called *the survival of the fittest*—a Darwinian mechanism of natural selection, only the emotionally mature understand this and do everything possible to avoid it. Such competitions only create anxiety, fear, and low self-esteem. Hence, billionaires avoid unhealthy comparisons and competitions.

You are doing yourself a great disservice to live a life of perpetual comparison. Do not compare yourself with certain people because you don't know their socio-economic level. Even if you know their socioeconomic level, you cannot be sure that what they portray outside is a true reflection of their lives. Remember, life is in phases, men are in sizes. Therefore, live your size per time.

Be Wise

As a matter of principle, make it your routine to learn to think about, study, and understand every situation before you act. Put another way, you must learn to put things

> *"Remember, life is in phases, men are in sizes. Therefore, live your size per time."*

in perspective before jumping to a conclusion. And if there is one area that the need to operate by this principle is more important, it is the area of financial management.

Many people make poor financial choices not necessarily because they are foolish or acting based on instincts, but because they do not understand some basic principles of the money game. In the realm of financial management, to be wise means to understand the operational principles of wealth creation and maintenance. And that is what this book is all about. The fact that you are still reading this book shows that you are on the right path to creating lasting wealth. Congratulations!

CHAPTER SUMMARY

- Moderation is not so much about how much one spends as it is about how much one spends in proportion to his income.
- When your expenses outweigh your income, you are living above your means.
- Billionaires avoid unhealthy comparisons and competitions.
- Make it your routine to learn to think about, study, and understand every situation before you act.
- In the realm of financial management, to be wise means to understand the operational principles of wealth creation and maintenance.

CHAPTER 11

CONSISTENT VENTURES

"Billionaires put the vast majority of their investment in ventures that have proven overtime to be consistent and have a high guarantee of returns."

— Dr. Stephen Akintayo

If you want to succeed in business, you must train yourself to understand the difference between investments that are consistent and those that are not. In other words, you must be able to distinguish between businesses that have high guarantee levels and those that do not. Billionaires can easily tell the difference between these two categories of investment; that is why they are always succeeding. While they may from time to time invest in businesses that have high profit but present great risk, billionaires put the vast majority of their investment in ventures that have proven overtime to be consistent and have a high guarantee of returns. This way, they can reduce the risk of loss to the barest minimum.

But poor people invest based on the spur of the moment. The investment habit of most people is determined by what is trending. It is not surprising that most new investment ventures always target poor people because they know that they are the ones who become easily carried away by the promise of quick returns for their money without minding or giving careful thought about whether a particular business venture has been known to be consistent over time or not.

"No matter how good and promising an investment may appear to be, never invest in something that you cannot substantiate and defend.

Ask for Evidence

No matter how good and promising an investment may appear to be, never invest in something that you cannot substantiate and defend. Always ask for proof or evidence of a business venture before putting your money into it. By evidence, I mean the need to verify and substantiate in concrete terms that the venture is not only genuine but also has the capacity to deliver on its promises. This is the billionaire's routine in approaching business. Hence, it is difficult to try to convince a billionaire to invest in something without first presenting him or her concrete proof of the success story of the investment alongside the nitty-gritty of the investment.

Billionaires only invest in real and consistent ventures. They do not invest in something based on hearsay or mere emotionalism. They must see a pattern of consistency in the business before they can even consider it. Here is a practical example that resonates: Bitcoin had been in existence for more than ten years and, for all those years, Elon Musk never spoke openly about it until late 2020. Why do you think that was so? It was probably because he had been asking questions privately about it for all those years until he started noticing a pattern of consistency and then decided to put his investment there. This is a common pattern among billionaires.

On many occasions, people ask me: "Dr. Akintayo, why do you put most of your money in real estate?" My simple answer to them is, as the name implies, real estate is the

"Billionaires only invest in real and consistent ventures. They do not invest in something based on hearsay or mere emotionalism."

only investment that is *real*. That is hyperbolic, but I say that to make a point. It does not mean that I don't invest in other ventures apart from real estate. I do. But most of my money goes to real estate because I have found it to be consistent, reliable, and tangible.

> *"Many people make the mistake of investing in businesses that they do not understand let alone try to substantiate their genuineness and authenticity."*

Many people make the mistake of investing in businesses that they do not understand let alone try to substantiate their genuineness and authenticity. It is such investment choices that end up making people delusional and apathetic about investment. Because they lack the patience to invest in things that they have found to be consistent and reliable, they end up losing a lot of their fortune and conclude that investment is a fraud.

Beware of Ponzi Schemes

When I was talking with one of my mentees in 2020, she said to me, "Oh, there's this investment I have made, and it promises great returns." I recall telling her that it was a sponsored Ponzi scheme without even probing further. But she said to me, "You don't need to worry about that. I've got it figured out. I have an insider; someone I know and trust. He tells me everything about it. By the way, I have been making money from it already." I was not surprised when she called after a couple of months to inform me that the owners of the business had disappeared. Upon hearing that, I just shook my head in wonder of how credulous and obstinate people could be about such things despite seeing all the warning signs. I believe she called me because she realized the futility of her decision and her refusal to heed my wise and experienced counsel. Instead of withdrawing her money immediately, she waited until everything dissipated. Curious, as if I could not decipher what had happened, I asked this mentee of mine, "Did you at least get your invested capital back?"Her response was, "No, I didn't." She continued, "I was reluctant about joining at first. When I finally decided to join, the scheme was on the verge of crashing."

Ponzi schemes have always had the same pattern. They start by promising their investors great returns. In the first few weeks or months, they collect money from their investors and give it as profit to the earliest investors. Because of the testimony of the first investors who are "lucky" to receive outrageous amounts of profits on their investment within a short time, they propagate and legitimize the scheme among their peers, friends, and family members. This brings about an influx of many people who invest with the hope of getting the same results. But by the time many people start investing, there is not enough money to circulate around as profit and the owners of the scheme are always smart enough to pack their belongings and disappear without a trace. This is the standard pattern of these fraudulent activities. But every time a new scheme appears, many naïve and nescient people rush to put their fortune there, or some buy time to see if it will last, then finally invest—never learning from history, ignoring the pattern.

Beware of Greed

Greed contributes to the poor investment choices and habits of most poor people. It is greed that makes people want to invest in ventures that will give them triple or quadruple returns of their investment within a short time. How would you feel if you can invest a thousand dollars and get five thousand from your investment within three weeks? Doesn't that sound fabulous and enticing? You can imagine how such an advertisement would appeal to poor people!

> *"It is greed that makes people want to invest in ventures that will give them triple or quadruple returns of their investment within a short time."*

Because of greed, people rush into such things thinking that they are acting smart. I am glad that I have never fallen victim to any Ponzi scheme. The reason is I have never allowed myself to be carried away by what is trending, especially if it looks too good to be true. Skepticism is also the billionaire's routine. You must learn to be skeptical about any investment that promises you two hundred percent, one hundred percent, fifty percent, and even fifteen percent. If such things were true, everyone would be rich.

Assuming someone tells you that there is a new investment company that gives investors great returns, you ask them, "What does the company do?" They tell you they trade on precious stones. Instead of saying, "Kindly take me to the company so I can see some of the precious stones that they have been trading in," you decide to blindly trust the report and use it as a parameter for your investment decision. A wise person who understands the investment habits of billionaires would

> *"It does not mean that billionaires are immune to greed. The only difference is that billionaires have learned to curtail their greed and allow logic to take precedence over their investment choices."*

want to know: Where is the company's refinery? Where is the trading taking place? For how long has this company been in existence? Who founded this company? To which country or proven entity is this company affiliated or registered? And so forth. But many people lack the patience to ask these questions. That is where greed comes in, and that is why it takes being greedy to fall victim to Ponzi schemes.

But billionaires are only going to invest in something real and proven to be consistent. It does not mean that billionaires are immune to greed. The only difference is that billionaires have learned to curtail their greed and allow logic to take precedence over their investment choices. That's their routine: logic over emotions and popular opinion. This explains why the rich will keep getting richer and the poor keep getting poorer. The remedy is a mind reset among poor people in terms of greed that often manifests itself in get-rich-quick schemes that are preponderant in many societies.

CHAPTER SUMMARY

- If you want to succeed in business, you must train yourself to understand the difference between investments that are consistent and those that are not.
- No matter how good and promising an investment may appear to be, never invest in something that you cannot substantiate and defend.
- Billionaires only invest in real and consistent ventures. They do not invest in something based on hearsay or mere emotionalism.
- It is greed that makes people want to invest in ventures that will give them triple or quadruple returns of their investment within a short time.
- Billionaires are not immune to greed. The only difference is that billionaires have learned to curtail their greed and allow logic to take precedence over their investment choices.

PART SEVEN

MENTORSHIP CODE

No one can succeed without a mentor. Every great person—a billionaire or not—has a mentor. It does not matter the field of vocational endeavor, people who go on to become great achievers are those who have willingly and carefully chosen mentors for themselves.

One of the cardinal arguments presented in this part is: If there is ever any shortcut to success, then it is mentorship. It allows you to stand on the shoulders of giants and achieve great things within a reasonably short time that personal, lone discovery would have taken decades to achieve. The Mentorship Code is captured in Chapter 12 which discusses the concept of *Mentored Partnerships.* It shows that billionaires never invest in any venture without due consultations with business mentors or partners.

MENTORED PARTNERSHIPS

"Billionaires value the opinion of experts."
– Dr. Stephen Akintayo

Billionaire investors have mentors and partners in every venture they embark upon. Because they are always surrounded by the right people who counsel, teach, guide, enlighten, and coach them about different forms of investment, they never invest their money in Ponzi schemes. It is difficult to see a billionaire become a victim of a Ponzi scheme; they are more likely to be the owners of the duplicitous investment scheme. Conversely, poor people tend to make wrong choices especially in areas of investment because they lack business mentors and partners who can guide them aright. The reasons for this are multifaceted, but most of them could be traced to ignorance about the operational framework of investment.

In short, many people do not know how to protect, manage, and multiply their money. Because they lack the right information, they keep losing money, getting frustrated, pessimistic, despondent, and nihilistic about life. In extreme cases, some go to the extent of committing suicide because of incessant financial predicaments. Many poor people watch passively and helplessly as poverty is perpetuated from one generation to the other in their lineage. The principles that we have been explicating in this book are meant to break such vicious circles and point people to the path of financial freedom. One of such principles is mentorship.

"In the game of investment, people who try to do it alone make a lot of blunders that they live to regret."

Eschew the Lone Game

Truly, no man is an island. In the game of investment, people who try to do it alone make a lot of blunders that they live to regret. No matter how smart and intelligent you think you are—except if you are an investment expert—taking the investment route without the counsel and guidance of experts may at the long run prove to be not only unwise but disastrous.

Even if you can't afford a mentor or don't have a business partner, there are many ways you can start this journey by learning from others. You can watch thousands of free videos online or at least read several books on the topic. But never be a lone gamer when it comes to investment. When Bill Gates was about to start investing and doing charity work in Nigeria, he decided to partner with Aliko Dangote. Why did Gates consider that decision important? Because he knew that working with someone who knows the system would save him a lot of headaches. He didn't have time to start learning about the Nigerian culture all by himself. He, therefore, made a smart choice by partnering with one of Africa's richest persons who happens to be a Nigerian. That is how billionaires approach business and investment. When it comes to investment, billionaires don't believe in a one-man show. They always involve others because they value the opinion of experts.

"When it comes to investment, billionaires don't believe in a one-man show. They always involve others because they value the opinion of experts."

Find a Mentor

Billionaires do not arrogate themselves to the point where they feel they don't need people to teach them anything. Contrariwise, the reason they are billionaires is that they have learned, over the years, to work effectively with many people thereby learning about the principles, methods, and challenges of investment. The more their wealth and riches grow and multiply, the more they continue to seek expert advice on a lot of things so they will be able to protect and maintain what they have worked hard to acquire. In other words, billionaires are perpetual learners. Because nothing is static in life, billionaires have trained themselves to be malleable based on the changing times.

"Because nothing is static in life, billionaires have trained themselves to be malleable based on the changing times."

In 2020, Elon Musk commented on a tweet by one of his friends that sent bitcoin into an automatic frenzy. His friend tweeted that he had invested up to a billion dollars in bitcoin and Elon Musk made a comment asking if someone could invest in bulk in the currency. When I saw that tweet, I knew immediately that Musk was going to invest in bitcoin. Billionaires will always find a mentor who will teach, guide, and coach them about the intricacies of an investment, or they will find themselves a business partner who is already in the business and understands it. Even when they are embarking on charity, they find themselves a mentor or partner just so they can do it the right way and avoid making costly mistakes.

There is a concept referred to as *institutional investor,* which is a financial entity that acquires money to purchase things such as securities, real property, and other investment assets. And sometimes, an institutional investor may originate loans. One of the powerful ways billionaires invest with a guarantee of not losing their money is through institutional investors. Through this process, they don't lose money even when they decide to do high-risk investments. Through institutional trading, when billionaires join a business, it automatically takes the price higher. For instance, shortly after Elon Musk decided to invest in bitcoin, the price of bitcoin skyrocketed overnight. Because he came in huge, that is, as an institution, he seemed to have legitimized bitcoin overnight.

> *"Because they lack the right information, they keep losing money, getting frustrated, pessimistic, despondent, and nihilistic about life."*

Since billionaires constantly ply the investment game like this, it's difficult for them to lose money through their investment to the extent of becoming broke. Being surrounded by financial experts who are their mentors and advisers, their chances of making investment blunders are drastically mitigated.

As the holy writ says, "Wisdom is profitable to direct!" So, you need a mentor. You need partners too; not only in the area of investments but in literally every field of endeavor.

CHAPTER SUMMARY

- Billionaire investors have mentors and partners in every venture they embark upon.
- In the game of investment, people who try to do it alone make a lot of blunders that they live to regret.
- When it comes to investment, billionaires don't believe in a one-man show. They always involve others because they value the opinion of experts.
- Because nothing is static in life, billionaires have trained themselves to be malleable based on the changing times.
- One of the powerful ways billionaires invest with a guarantee of not losing their money is through institutional investors.

PART EIGHT

THINKING CODE

Becoming rich is a mind game. Thoughts control and inform everything we do. Billionaires have disciplined thought patterns that enable them visualize a goal and follow through to achieve it. They do not achieve great things because they are the brightest or the most talented. They are able to do so because they have disciplined thought patterns and pay the price for information and knowledge.

We often think of investment only in terms of money and possessions. The Thinking Code emphasizes the importance of investing in knowledge and then using that acquired knowledge to achieve great things. Chapter 13, *Invested Knowledge*, explains that one of the most important investments you can make is an investment in knowledge. You will learn that the knowledge of an investment opportunity is more important than the investment itself.

INVESTED KNOWLEDGE

"A smart investor is someone who takes time to investigate and ask relevant questions about an investment before venturing into it."

– Dr. Stephen Akintayo

You may be familiar with the saying "knowledge is power." But I want to modify it slightly to say knowledge only becomes power when it is properly applied. When it comes to investment, the knowledge of an investment opportunity is more important than the investment itself. It was Benjamin Franklin, one of the founding fathers of the United States of America, who once said, "An investment in knowledge pays the best interest."

This is one of the investment habits of billionaires: They invest in the knowledge of an investment before the investment itself. In other words, billionaires learn all they can and understudy a particular investment that they are interested in before deciding whether it is worth it. They would rather take their time and, if need be, spend money to learn about the investment in order to decide whether it is the right fit for them.

But poor people do the opposite. When they hear about an investment from a friend, family member, or colleague at work, they are always unhesitant to put their money into it despite not understanding the operational framework of the investment. The people who create Ponzi schemes understand this attitude of poor people and therefore make them their hapless targets. Billionaires never fall prey to Ponzi schemes. But poor people do over and again.

"As a rule of thumb, any investment that seems too good to be true is probably a fake."

Don't Rush

One of the factors that lead to poor investment choices is impatience—a sense of urgency that says if you don't invest now, you are going to lose. Some investments, especially counterfeit ones, pressurize people to put their money into something they have little or no knowledge about, quickly! As a rule of thumb, any investment that seems too good to be true is probably a fake. Unfortunately, it is this sense of urgency that often makes poor people invest in things the *modus operandi* of which

"When it comes to investment, the knowledge of an investment opportunity is more important than the investment itself."

they do not understand. But billionaires would rather hold back, wait, and patiently learn about a potential investment. Hence, billionaires' investment risks and losses are drastically reduced compared to the losses of people who rush into an investment without knowing what it is about.

If you want to become a billionaire or succeed in your business, rushing to invest is never a shortcut. Anytime you realize that you are rushing to invest in something just because someone has told you about it, but you don't understand how it works, it is better to halt and try to find out more about it. Don't invest because of instincts or emotions, for if you do, you are most likely to regret it in the future.

One of my mentees once told me about an investment program that she was interested in and wanted to put her money into. When I tried to inquire what she knew about the investment, I realized that she had not done her homework. She only heard about it and wanted to try it because she thought that it had good prospects. I tried to dissuade her, but I couldn't tell whether she heeded my warning. And the sad thing about such investment is that when an expert tries to warn people that are about to rush into it, such expert will be termed a skeptic or an ignoramus. Even when such people come seeking your advice, they have already made up their minds to go ahead. It is like they have already presumed your response, but they just wanted to confirm it and afterward go ahead with their plans. An expert's caution about such things is often overlooked. Such people will seem to have it all figured out. In the end, they'd wish they had the patience to carry out due diligence.

> *"Don't invest because of instincts or emotions, for if you do, you are most likely to regret it in the future."*

Seek Knowledge

Always invest in the knowledge of a business before investing in the business itself. But what most people do is invest in the business before trying to understand it. In fact, many poor people only know about an investment opportunity after they have lost money in it. This explains why most poor people often end up losing the money they have earned a hundred times over. Until you train yourself to acquire knowledge, you will keep losing your money in investments because you lack the patience to learn, research, and understand it.

Here is a practical example: If a billionaire wants to invest in cryptocurrency, he will first invest in understanding what cryptocurrency is about. From there, he will be able to analyze and synthesize the pros and cons of such investment and decide appropriately. Even if the investment requires a great amount of risk, the billionaire is not ignorant about the risk involved and so he does not invest blindly.

But this is how a poor person will approach the same thing: He will put his money in cryptocurrency first before trying to learn what it is about. This difference in investment habits, amongst other things, accounts for why the poor keep getting poorer and the rich keep getting richer. A poor man may argue thus, "If I spend ten thousand dollars learning about cryptocurrency, where will I get the money to make the investment? I would rather take that money (which happens to be my entire savings) and put it in cryptocurrency and trust God that it will work out

"many poor people only know about an investment opportunity after they have lost money in it. This explains why most poor people often end up losing the money they have earned a hundred times over."

well. I may not understand how it works, but I cannot afford to give my entire savings to someone to teach me about cryptocurrency." The illogicality of such an argument is that it fails to take into consideration the fact that it is not really the money one invests in cryptocurrency that is the most important but the knowledge of cryptocurrency itself.

Let me reiterate that if you want to start investing as billionaires do, you must learn to understand what you are putting your money into. That is the first and right step toward investment.

Check Track Record

When people approach me saying they want to do business with me, the first thing I want to know is their track record. Have they attempted a similar thing before? If so, did they succeed or fail? However, when people approach me with such requests, they often say things like: "Can you invest in my business?" "I need 50 million Naira from you to start my business." The question that readily comes to mind is: Where's your track record? What is the proof that you are the right person to engage in this business? Do you plan on using my money to experiment in a business that you know little or nothing about?

The same principle applies to investment. Before you invest in anything, you need to check the track record of the business organization and the people that are in charge. Failure to investigate and pay attention to track records is one of the reasons many poor people make wrong investment choices and suffer the consequences, saying things like, "It was my friend who deceived me to invest with them." "It was because of the caliber of people that I saw there that convinced me to invest. I didn't know it was going to end like this."

> *"A smart investor is someone who takes time to investigate and ask relevant questions about an investment before venturing into it."*

Billionaires don't invest simply because they have seen their friends, family members, or people they trust invest. It is never about who is asking them to invest. They invest based on the knowledge they have about the investment. They don't care whether the richest man in the world is also investing in that venture. The way they play the game is totally different. They invest based on knowledge and conviction. That way, they are willing to take responsibility for whatever happens—either gain or loss.

But poor people like to follow the crowd. They observe what everyone is doing and they join the bandwagon. Because they lack knowledge and skills in this area, they think they will be cheated if they do not join the new trend in town. That is not the way billionaires think. A smart investor is someone who takes time to investigate and ask relevant questions about an investment before venturing into it. And one of the most important questions to ask relates to track record.

Here is a practical example of the importance of checking people's and company's track record before investing in anything. Two years ago, we were planning to launch an estate and the money we had was below our estimated budget. We, therefore, decided to do a pre-launch so we could make up the difference. We had already signed an agreement with the sellers but had only half of the cost. Our idea of doing a pre-launch was to ask people to pay for the property at the same price we were buying from the sellers so that we could pay the owners before making profit later. So, we told people: If you are investing before the day of the launch, you will not see the estate because we have not launched it yet. But if you can trust us enough to give us your money, we are going to give you a fifty percent discount. To our

"You too can build a track record to make people trust you with their money. It is all about doing what you say you will do."

amazement, we were able to raise over 100 million naira in two weeks. Why did these people trust our company and decide to give us money when they had not even seen the estate? It was because of our track record. And that has become our pattern. They knew we had done several of such things in the past and stood by our word. Therefore, they had no reason to doubt whether we were going to keep to our word this time.

Use OPM

OPM stands for *Other People's Money*. Billionaires have learnt to use other people's money to make meaningful investments. In the game of investment, you have two choices: You can either use your personal money or OPM. Smart billionaires always end up using other people's money because they have a good track record and people do not hesitate to trust them with their money. You too can build a track record to make people trust you with their money. It is all about doing what you say you will do. When using OPM, you need to make sure you understand the business and you do not lose people's money. This is where people often err. They use OPM in investments that they are not ready to study. In the end, they suffer loss and build a bad reputation for themselves. When billionaires decide to use OPM, they do everything possible to never disappoint the people from whom they borrowed the money.

But someone may say, "Billionaires can use OPM because people know that they (the billionaires asking people to invest) have plenty of money and they (the investors) will always get their money back no matter what happens." While such an argument may sound logical, it is not always true that if you are not rich, people are not going to entrust their money into your hands. The major problem that hinders people from attracting other people's money is that they are not sure of themselves; and because of that, people are not sure of what they can do. Simply, they don't have any track record, no matter how small, to prove that they know what they are doing. Who would want to entrust their resources to someone who has not proven his worth in anything? There is no track record or evidence that you have been trained. If people suspect that you don't know what you are talking about, they cannot trust you with their resources. To win people's trust, you must have a good track record. And a good track record is not limited to previous investments. It may just mean that people want to see some evidence that you have the right knowledge of what you are talking about. This concept is expanded more in Chapter 24.

This, you see, is how billionaires thrive: They invest in knowledge, not just of investments, but of every other thing affecting them, grow their minds to the point where they can make informed and responsible decisions, and be confidently accountable for their choices. To grow in your thoughts is to grow in life. So invest in knowledge, challenge your current thinking patterns, especially the ones which keep leading to defeating outcomes. Unless you learn to do something differently, you'll keep getting the same results. That said, an investment in knowledge is crucial.

CHAPTER SUMMARY

- When it comes to investment, the knowledge of an investment opportunity is more important than the investment itself.
- As a rule of thumb, any investment that seems too good to be true is probably fake.
- Before you invest in anything, you need to check the track record of the business organization and the people that are in charge.
- A smart investor is someone who takes time to investigate and ask relevant questions about an investment before venturing into it.
- Billionaires thrive by investing in knowledge, not just of investments, but of every other thing affecting them, grow their minds to the point where they can make informed and responsible decisions, and be confidently accountable for their choices.

PART NINE

EFFECTIVENESS CODE

An institution—business or otherwise—that can be considered effective must be built with sustainability in mind. Thus whether the owner is there or not, with or without personal supervision, the system works. Billionaires, just like all people, have only twenty-four hours in a day. Therefore, to achieve their ambitious goals, to leave behind effective systems, they discipline themselves to consciously choose and pay attention to impotant things like conscious mentorship.

Chapter 14 shows how billionaires build and sustain effective systems through the principle of replication: first, their mindset; next, they replicate proven principles. Thus, ensuring sustainability.

REPLICATION PRINCIPLE

"Leaders who build effective systems raise people who think, act, and approach life and business like them."
– Dr. Stephen Akintayo

When billionaires are ready to multiply their wealth, they follow the principle of replication. In business, the replication principle deals with the conscious repetition of a validated success so that it can continue to generate growth and expansion. Billionaires apply the replication principle in two major ways.

> *"In business, the replication principle deals with the conscious repetition of a validated success so that it can continue to generate growth and expansion."*

Firstly, they multiply themselves in others. They make sure that they intentionally mentor other people by pouring out their wealth of experience on them. Through many years of experience—years of successes and failures, pains and gains, excitements and disappointments—they have understood and applied life principles that are not taught in formal academic settings. Knowing this, they intentionally mentor and coach other people of like minds to follow and apply these principles for maximum success in life.

Secondly, they replicate their businesses. Billionaires do not only seek to replicate their life principles to help others succeed, they also try to replicate their business models in different ventures for maximum growth and expansion. By using the same work principles in different business settings,

"A principle, by definition, is a proven way of life that can be applied under any given circumstances to produce desired results."

they keep sharpening and strengthening those principles to make them relevant and applicable under any business setting.

A principle, by definition, is a proven way of life that can be applied under any given circumstances to produce desired results. Ray Dalio, an American billionaire businessman, hedge fund manager, founder of Bridgewater Associates, and author of the bestselling book, *Principles,* emphasizes that "Principles are fundamental truths that serve as the foundation for behavior that gets you what you want out of life. They can be applied again and again in similar situations to help you achieve your goals." He goes further to explain that "All successful people operate by principles that help them be successful, though what they choose to be successful at varies enormously, so their principles vary."

Replicate Yourself in Others

Someone once said that you are yet to start living until you have replicated yourself in the life of another person. One of the major regrets that rich, famous, and influential people often have toward the end of their lives is the failure to replicate

"One of the major regrets that rich, famous, and influential people often have toward the end of their lives is the failure to replicate themselves in other people."

themselves in other people. No matter how vast the wealth or businesses you have acquired or built, someday you will be no more. And when you are gone, other people will take charge of all the things you have worked hard to accumulate. When that happens, your successors may either expand those businesses or crumble them. To avoid a scenario whereby shortly after you are gone, everything you have worked hard to achieve automatically dissipates, you must be conscious and determined to replicate yourself in the lives of other people whom you would want to take after you. These may be your family members (spouse, children, siblings, or distant relatives), trusted business colleagues, or just anyone that you have an interest in grooming. Anyone who fails to intentionally replicate himself in the life of another person is most likely to be soon forgotten.

Come to think of it, what is the essence of building something that will not last? What is the essence of building a business empire that will come crumbling down as soon as you are no longer on the scene? That doesn't make any sense. Billionaires usually build their businesses with sustainability in mind. The best way to achieve this is by building a system that works without the direct supervision of the billionaire. This means that the billionaire consciously sets up a system that ensures that the desired results for the business are gotten while under the supervision of other competent and committed caretakers.

Our GText company, for instance, has just openedan office in Dubai. There is a Nigerian lady living in Dubai whom I have, over the years, come to trust. Because I have been mentoring her for quite some time now and have tried to replicate myself in her, it was easy for me to assign her the herculean responsibility of running our GText Dubai office. Despite that, after opening the office, I still had to stay in Dubai for a month to coach her about certain principles of running a business such as ours. I want her to be able to think about business the way I do so she can contribute immensely to GText's effectiveness and growth in Dubai.

Through intentional mentoring and coaching, our new administrative staff in Dubai will be able to replicate my life and work principles even in my absence. When I leave, I don't have to stress myself about the daily running of our Dubai office because I know that I have put someone in charge who can operate the business the way I would do it myself. The same principle applies to our Abuja, United States, and United Kingdom offices. Some people must run those offices. The most important thing I need to do is to make sure that I have replicated myself in those people so they can have the life and work principles similar to mine. But this cannot happen by chance. It must involve a conscious effort on my part to train and mentor others to think and approach business the way I do.

Unfortunately, most people are often hesitant to share the secrets of their lives and businesses with others. They prefer to hide from others the principles they use to achieve success. Such people wrongly assume that teaching, mentoring, and coaching others to use the same systems they use would result in those people overtaking them. Therefore, they hide those systems and principles from others so that no one will be able to replicate what they do. When they find a particular life or business principle to be beneficial, they do everything possible to hide it from others. These kinds of people cannot build lasting wealth because once they leave the scene, what they have built alone will crumble since no one was taught the secrets that helped the business grow.

To live and die well, you must learn to replicate yourself in others, except if that which you want to replicate is not going to benefit them positively. This is an important distinction to make because so many people often prefer to replicate their negative experiences in the lives of others. If they try something and fail, they also want others to go through the same thing and experience the pain they have experienced. Such replication efforts are at best detrimental and ill-conceived.

Grow by Replication

If you know something and refuse to teach it to others in the guise of not wanting anyone to know what your success secrets are, you are stunting your growth and the potential of grooming other people that will replicate your principles for the betterment of society. This is why many people never scale their businesses. For you to scale your business, you must replicate your life and business principles in others. There is a dimension of what you know and who you are that you must pour into other people. If you are sure that other people will represent you well and do what you are doing to succeed in life and business, then there is no reason for you to refuse to share. Under such circumstances, refusing to share may be considered selfishness.

"For you to scale your business, you must replicate your life and business principles in others. There is a dimension of what you know and who you are that you must pour into other people."

"To live and die well, you must learn to replicate yourself in others, except if that which you want to replicate is not going to benefit them positively."

One of the people I respect the most in this area is Tony Elumelu, the Nigerian economist, entrepreneur, philanthropist, and Founder of the Tony Elumelu Foundation. His Foundation was established "based on the belief that, with the right support, entrepreneurs can be empowered to contribute meaningfully to Africa's prosperity and social development." One of Elumelu's powerful secrets is his ability to replicate himself in people. As such, he does not struggle to have good, competent, and amazing people working for him. That is a skill anyone who desires to multiply his business must endeavor to have. With the way Elumelu has been a trailblazer in the area of entrepreneurship and philanthropy in Africa, I believe that in no distant time he is most likely to become the richest man in Africa. The reason for such a projection is not implausible: Elumelu has an unequal ability to replicate leaders—and great leaders for that matter. He is conscious and determined about the way he goes about mentoring, coaching, teaching, and replicating his kind all over Africa. The Tony Elumelu Foundation gives grants to people all over Africa and that has been applauded by many renowned Africans and people all over the world. There is no doubt that Elumelu knows how to look for great leaders, employ them, engage them, and get them to work toward a particular course.

If you must replicate your money, that is, if you plan to multiply your income, you must imbibe the principle of replication. It is one of the secrets that billionaires use to increase their wealth and influence. They first replicate themselves—their mindsets—in other people before they replicate their business principles. This is because they understand that it is people that will help grow or destroy the business and this is determined largely by the mindset of the people. Therefore, it is better to first replicate the mindset that has helped you become a billionaire in the people under you before teaching them the principles.

"You replicate yourself in other people so they can act, think, behave, and approach life and business like you."

From 2021, we are replicating GText Homes in Dubai, the United States, and the United Kingdom. My ability as a billionaire to replicate my life and business principles in other people—to open them up to the level of what I know, what I think, and how I think—is particularly important for the success of our GText companies in those various locations. If I do not become vulnerable with them to that extent, it will be difficult for them to run the businesses in those locations successfully.

Consequently, I will not be able to keep replicating and enjoying that level of success personally.

Suffice it to say that the practice of vulnerability with one's life and business principles is quite challenging, but it is not unattainable. A billionaire has the responsibility to replicate not only himself in other people but also replicate the model of the business. You replicate yourself in other people so they can act, think, behave, and approach life and business like you. This is one of the key characteristics of billionaires who have been able to build successful businesses.

Have you ever wondered why Apple has continued to thrive after the death of Steve Jobs? It is because Jobs was able to replicate himself in Tim Cook. Jobs replicated his personal business philosophy and Apple culture in Cook to the extent that there is no glaring difference between their leadership patterns. That is why Apple has continued to be successful. It is operating with proven principles that were established and taught by Jobs, its visionary leader. Leaders who build effective systems raise people who think, act, and approach life and business like them.

CHAPTER SUMMARY

- Billionaires apply the replication principle in two major ways; they replicate themselves in people and then replicate their businesses.
- No matter how vast the wealth or businesses you have acquired or built, someday you will be no more. And when you are gone, other people will take charge of all the things you have worked hard to accumulate.
- For you to scale your business, you must replicate your life and business principles in others. There is a dimension of what you know and who you are that you must pour into other people.
- It is better to first replicate the mindset that has helped you become a billionaire in the people under you before teaching them the principles.
- You replicate yourself in other people so they can act, think, behave, and approach life and business like you.

PART TEN

VOLUME CODE

Adistinguishing code for billionaires' success and massive wealth is their volume. The more services you provide, the more rewards you are likely to gain. This is the law of the universe. Your ability to multiply whatever you are paid to do determines your success in business. That is what drives the idea of the volume code.

You may be good and skillful at what you do, but until you know how to apply the volume code, you may end up becoming mediocre in your business. This concept is expounded in Chapters 15, *Business Volume*, and Chapter 16, *Multiple Businesses*, which explains the principle that billionaires use to own multiple businesses and succeed at them.

CHAPTER 15

BUSINESS VOLUME

"Speed is only useful if you're running in the right direction."
– Joel Barker

Billionaires always start with services before moving to products. But the mere transitioning to products is not enough to make a business succeed. Therefore, they use the principle of volume to scale their businesses. Business volume means the quantity of products that are circulated at any given time. More specifically, it deals with the quantity of products that a company

"Business volume means the quantity of products that are circulated at any given time. More specifically, it deals with the quantity of products that a company produces, sells, and makes profits from at any given time.

produces, sells, and makes profits from at any given time. The demand for volume can come from personal or group needs.

Volume is what makes businesses scale and become billion-dollar companies. Amazon, for instance, is a trillion-dollar company because of its volume. With close to a million employees, Amazon leverages volume to outdo every online business company in the world through the products and services it provides to people in many parts of the world.

> *"In the world of business, numbers speak more than any other factor. The tests of validation and consumption reveal your numbers and help you decide whether you are ready for volume or not."*

It is important to stress out that billionaires do not start with volume. In other words, they do not randomly create a product in a million quantity and start selling. The strategy they use is to first test the product in the market space to ascertain whether it is going to fly. As the saying goes, "Nothing can really happen until someone sells something." To know whether your product is ready to have volume, it must first pass the test of validation and consumption. The test of validation relates to the number of people that are talking about the uniqueness of the product. The test of consumption has to do with the number of people who have bought the product and found it to be useful. In the world of business, numbers speak more than any other factor. The tests of validation and consumption reveal your numbers and help you decide whether you are ready for volume or not.

The Law of Demand and Supply

Business volume rests upon two key factors: demand and supply. The law of demand states that "Quantity purchased varies inversely with price." In other words, the higher the price of a product, the lower the quantity that will be demanded. Conversely, the lower the price of a product, the higher the demand. Practically, then, if you want to maximize volume in your business, you must pay attention to the law of demand; that is, how expensive your product is compared to other products in the market. You must learn to pay attention to not only the need for the product but also to its affordability in the market space.

The law of supply, on the other hand, states that "All other factors being equal, as the price of a good or service increases, the quantity of goods or services that suppliers offer will

> *"You must learn to pay attention to not only the need for the product but also to its affordability in the market space."*

increase, and vice versa." In other words, the higher the price of a product, the more the suppliers will want to increase the volume of the product to maximize profit.

Both the law of demand and the law of supply are important variables to pay attention to before you increase the volume of your business. If you ignore these key factors and go about increasing your business volume based on instincts or assumptions, you are likely to accrue losses if it turns out that your assumptions were wrong. That is why it is important to pay attention to demand and supply before you apply

"Never make assumptions about the quality and demand of your product and use that assumption to increase its volume."

the principle of volume in your business. As Joel Barker puts it, "Speed is only useful if you're running in the right direction." Therefore, never make assumptions about the quality and demand of your product and use that assumption to increase its volume. Have the patience to study the facts, for facts never lie.

Higher demand for a product in the market is always a good sign that the product is ready to scale using volume. This is why understanding the laws of demand and supply will help you to make informed and more accurate decisions about volume. Billionaires take the time to study these market forces well before making investments in volumes. They don't mind if this takes years. They are never in a hurry.

Here is a practical example that will buttress this point. I do a lot of paid coaching for people. One of my students in my coaching program wanted to scale his transportation business and needed my help. He told me he wanted to transform his transportation business into a particular product. He got the product at a cheap price and had an exclusive deal with the manufacturer. He had set aside fifty million naira for the product, but he wanted to share it with me first before signing the deal. After listening to him and asking key questions, I thought that the decision was not a smart one given the amount of volume he wanted to start the business with. So, I counseled him on the contrary. I told him, "I would advise you to hold on with the volume. It doesn't mean that putting that huge amount into the product may not bring great returns, but you need to test-run the product first in the market with a small amount. Doing that will help you make an informed decision based on the reality of demand and supply." I specifically advised him to start with one million naira rather than putting fifty million naira into something he was not yet sure about. I probably would have told him to start with a hundred thousand naira or less had he not told me about the fifty million that he was willing to put into the business.

Because billionaires often start with referrals, they start with good capital that enables them to scale faster and increase the volume of their business much sooner than others who start small. But remember that they first have to sacrifice by working for others and gaining capital to be able to start well. The reason many poor people start small is they never have people that will guide, coach, or mentor them in business. Most importantly, they do not start as a service. They are always thinking about products, not services. And even when they want to start with a product,

"Because billionaires often start with referrals, they start with good capital that enables them to scale faster and increase the volume of their business much sooner than others who start small."

they always seem to be in haste that they hardly take time to do feasibility studies to take into cognizance such variables as demand and supply. In the end, they don't have enough capital to scale, and they fail to have volume because they never have time to test the idea in the market space.

CHAPTER SUMMARY

- Volume is what makes businesses scale and become billion-dollar companies.
- In the world of business, numbers speak more than any other factor. The tests of validation and consumption reveal your numbers and help you decide whether you are ready for volume or not.
- Business volume rests upon two key factors: demand and supply.
- Higher demand for a product in the market is always a good sign that the product is ready to scale using volume.
- Because billionaires often start with referrals, they start with good capital that enables them to scale faster and increase the volume of their business much sooner than others who start small.

CHAPTER 16

MULTIPLE BUSINESSES

"This is a key principle about the billionaire mindset: Engage in multiple businesses, but focus only on one thing at a time."

– Dr Stephen Akintayo

Change, they say, is the only constant thing in life. One of the characteristics of contemporary societies is the reality of life being in a constant state of flux. Billionaires understand the reality of change and are constantly adjusting themselves and their businesses to meet up contemporary trends and demands. Not only do billionaires study and adapt to change, but they are also not restricted by fear. Billionaires are never afraid to try new things, but they do so with caution and carefulness.

One of the ways to become a billionaire is to be adventurous enough to try new things. People who are not afraid to try new things often discover certain gifts and capabilities that they had not previously thought they had, and with such realizations often come business ideas that expands and multiplies their financial status.

In short, billionaires own multiple businesses. This is one of their secrets to success. To build wealth, you must be willing to try new things even if it means going into unknown territory. But you don't go into an unknown territory unadvisedly. Never be afraid to try new things because you may never know what specific idea could become your business breakthrough.

> *"Billionaires often concentrate on one business, build it into a brand, before diverging into other ventures."*

While most billionaires own multiple businesses, they are often known for only one thing. In the discussion that follows, I will explain the principle that billionaires use to own multiple businesses and succeed at them. It is not as if they start their entrepreneurial journey by dabbling their hands into different things all at the same time. Billionaires often concentrate on one business, build it into a brand, before diverging into other ventures.

"Billionaires are never afraid to try new things, but they do so with caution and carefulness."

Don't Be the Jack of All Trades

Billionaires are often known by or associated with one specific business venture which is considered their signature business. At the same time, they never limit themselves to one thing. They are always thinking about expansion. Therefore, they often end up owning multiple businesses. But while they may own multiple businesses, most billionaires usually choose to focus on one.

Here is a practical example. Bill Gates is popularly known as the founder of Microsoft, but not many people know that he owns not less than 100 businesses. But how does he manage to succeed at these businesses? His secret is simple: He did not try to start multiple businesses all at the same time. Gates spent at least two decades building Microsoft to become a world brand before he considered owning other businesses.

> *"It is only after becoming a brand and building a certain level of wealth that billionaires diversify and start other businesses."*

But that is where many poor people get it mixed up. They think of the concept of multiple businesses as a fancy catchphrase and do not understand how people who become successful business owners play the game. So, they jump into starting multiple businesses all at the same time and later discover that they have become Jacks of all trades, masters of none. Billionaires always focus on one business, which usually grows to become their breakthrough business. And that breakthrough business becomes the signature business that everybody associates them with. However, they often invest in multiple other businesses. It is only after becoming a brand and building a certain level of wealth that billionaires diversify and start other businesses.

That is a key principle to always keep in mind when it comes to owning multiple businesses. Never trade quantity for quality. By this I mean, do not be tempted to start multiple businesses at the same time and expect them to be productive. If you are considering starting multiple businesses, you must first concentrate your energy, time, and resources on something that you do well and grow it to a strong financial stronghold before thinking of diversifying. Remember, where energy goes, energy flows. What you give most attention to multiplies. But if you divide your attention too soon into different businesses, you may end up having multiple good business ideas, but none of them may succeed.

For example, when Jeff Bezos—the richest person in the world at the point of writing this book—resigned as the CEO of Amazon in 2020, he was asked what he would be doing after his resignation. His answer was that he wanted to focus on the other smaller businesses that he owns.

"Remember, where energy goes, energy flows. What you give most attention to multiplies."

Can you see how billionaires think? The founder and CEO of a multi-billion-dollar company resign from his position to focus on other small businesses that he owns that are not currently well-known.

But when a poor man starts a potable water business today, instead of concentrating all his efforts to build it up until it becomes his breakthrough company, he wants to run a car business and other businesses all at the same time. That is why many poor people who start a business fail. They often lack the patience to concentrate on one thing, specialize, and be known for it, before moving to other things. In the end, because they have many hot irons in the fire, all of them burn.

Because most poor people who start a business lack this basic understanding of the operational principles of having a specialized and branded business before diversifying into other areas, they are always frustrated and ineffective since they put their hands in too many things without succeeding in any of them. This may explain why such people are always receiving multiple phone calls about different things that make them confused and inefficient. In fact, most of such people are likely to develop high blood pressure because of a lack of concentration in one thing.

The other day, I was talking with one of my friends who has been a partner in our company. He needed something in one of our properties that he is a contractor for. He approached me directly about it. What I did was to redirect him to the appropriate people in our GText company—the accountants and other operation managers that handle such cases. At first, he seemed bewildered that I had to direct him somewhere while I could help him directly as a friend. I had to make him understand that this is not how I operate my businesses.

If I decide to know and monitor all the money that comes into the companies that I manage, I will drop dead because I can't keep up. But that is typically what poor people do. Poor people want to engage themselves in too many things at the same time and the resultant consequences are confusion and inefficiency. They are always chasing shadows because they want to oversee everything to the detriment of their mental and psychological well-being. That is why they often end up unproductive and frustrated because of the divergent demands of the many

> *"Poor people want to engage themselves in too many things at the same time and the resultant consequences are confusion and inefficiency."*

unsuccessful things that they seem to be chasing all at once.

When it comes to employment, a poor man may have a good-paying full-time job, but instead of concentrating on that job and giving it his best while saving along the way, he may be tempted to get involved in other separate businesses. Because he is not focusing on his job and giving it his best, he might get fired because of inefficiency. And what becomes of his other businesses? They all collapse because he does not have the emotional temerity and financial capital to sustain them. He has become a hapless person who lost a fortune because of impatience and too many unnecessary distractions. Such are the kinds of mistakes that poor people often make because of a misunderstanding of the concept of having multiple streams of income.

Billionaires own multiple businesses, but they only focus on one that is their breakthrough business. Aliko Dangote, for instance, is the owner of multiple businesses. But Dangote does not run all his businesses. He is smart enough to know that doing so will constitute a huge distraction to him. So, what he does is

"This is a key principle about the billionaire mindset: Engage in multiple businesses, but focus only on one thing at a time."

concentrate on one aspect of his business at a time while he appoints many CEOs and managers to handle his other businesses. Right now, it seems as if his major focus is on the refinery he is building. That is where his attention is fully concentrated. Does it mean that he neglects his other businesses like Dangote Cement and Dangote Flour? Certainly not! He knows about their operations, but he has put many capable hands in those areas that he does not have to worry about what is going on there. This is a key principle about the billionaire mindset: Engage in multiple businesses, but focus only on one thing at a time.

Most poor people only have one source of income, but they try to do many things at the same time. In the end, everything suffers. One business principle that I have always taught the people I coach is that if you are an employee— if you have a good job—then focus on your job and make sure that you save enough from your salary and find a way to set up a business that does not require that you run it. That is the way to keep your current job and still be able to have another source of income coming into your bank account. But if you try to concentrate on different things that are demanding your attention, you may end up losing all. Never chase multiple things at the same time without having one that is stable.

"if you rush into too many businesses too soon without being known for anything, people are likely to perceive you as someone who lacks focus or is too ambitious."

Choose a Niche

To avoid the temptation of starting multiple businesses prematurely, it is important that you carve out a niche for yourself and work hard to see that you are known for it. Doing so opens you up to the world and establishes your credibility. When the world recognizes you as someone who has done something credible, it becomes much easier for people to trust you when you eventually decide to venture into other niches. The reason is, they know that you have done something incredible before, and they have little or no doubt that you can do it again. But if you rush into too many businesses too soon without being known for anything, people are likely to perceive you as someone who lacks focus or is too ambitious.

Choosing a niche does not necessarily mean building companies like Microsoft, Amazon, Apple, or Google. It just means whatever you set out to do, give it your absolute best and work hard to be known as someone who does it better than others. That is the credibility test that makes billionaires succeed. For instance, after passing the credibility test in founding Microsoft and

"Billionaires do not put all their eggs in one basket when it comes to business. They always have a specific niche they are known for, but it does not stop them from trying other businesses in other unrelated niches."

building it to become a brand, in 2006 Bill Gates became one of the major owners of *Four Seasons Hotels and Resorts*, having nearly fifty percent of the equity of the company. This is just one among many such businesses that Bill Gates owns. But many people around the world know him as the founder of Microsoft. While Gates' name has come to be regarded as almost synonymous with Microsoft, he has refused to cage himself in Microsoft despite its huge success as a company. What is his secret for success in other business ventures that seem totally unrelated to his technology company? The answer is obvious: It is because he has created a niche for himself that speaks for him anywhere he goes.

Billionaires do not put all their eggs in one basket when it comes to business. They always have a specific niche they are known for, but it does not stop them from trying other businesses in other unrelated niches. That is why they may be known as

"The world of business operates on the principle of branding. A brand, by definition, is a specific signature by which a business is known."

founders of a technology company and still have the leverage to own hotel or food businesses. A billionaire may build a niche for himself in real estate, but he may also own businesses in aviation, sports, e-commerce, and technology. The point I have been trying to make is that billionaires embrace the concept of having multiple businesses because they see it as a way of expansion and growth. They are never afraid to try something new. But they only do so after a huge breakthrough in a specific niche.

Become a Brand

Choosing a niche for yourself is not enough to catapult your business into wealth and establish credibility for you. When you have a niche, you must be determined to work hard to

"The most important thing is not so much the kind of brand you want to build but your resilience and persistence to build the brand."

become a brand. The world of business operates on the principle of branding. A brand, by definition, is a specific signature by which a business is known. It always has an identifying symbol, sign, mark, logo, name, word, mantra, or mode of operation. For instance, companies like McDonald's, Nike, Starbucks, Google, Apple, and Facebook are world brands. Brands are often used to distinguish one product from another. But there are also national brands, regional brands, geographical brands, state brands, ethnic brands, and local brands. And brands can be in every kind of venture. You can have a cloth brand, music brand, church brand, comedy skit brand, talk show brand, writing brand, and anything imaginable.

The most important thing is not so much the kind of brand you want to build but your resilience and persistence to build the brand. This is because many people who want to start a business often lack the patience and resilience to stick to it long enough to make it a brand. They start a business today and after a couple of months, if the results don't seem to be what they had envisaged, they abandon it and start another one. At other times, they rush into starting multiple businesses without specializing in any.

The world of business thrives on brands. Therefore, every billionaire is a brand. When your business grows to become a brand, people can develop a sense of cultic loyalty to what you offer them. Have you ever wondered why some people are so attached to certain computers, phones, cars, clothes, shoes, watches, churches, and music brands? The reason is, they have become accustomed to such brands that they are willing to pay anything just to have that brand. This is how the concept of brand loyalty—the positive loyalty that customers attach to certain brands—is used in business. If you are lucky to grow your business to a brand loyalty status, you have a stable business. At

> *"When your business grows to become a brand, people can develop a sense of cultic loyalty to what you offer them."*

that point, considering other business ventures will not cause any harm to your breakthrough business.

As such, when billionaires become a brand, they do not limit themselves to one thing. They begin to have invested interest in multiple businesses. But they do not do so at the detriment of other businesses they own. Take Elon Musk for instance, he came into the business world by co-founding PayPal, an electronic payment system company. But today, he is the CEO of Tesla and Space-X. Musk and his partner sold PayPal for about two billion dollars and used his part of the money to start Tesla and later Space-X. And most recently, he has invested a lot in bitcoin.

Billionaires own multiple businesses. However, they focus on one business and make sure it has grown before they use it as a base for going into other businesses. They may generally be associated with their breakthrough businesses, but not many people usually know that they are shareholders in many other businesses.

However, poor people who try to start multiple businesses all at once often miss this point. Because they learn that billionaires own multiple businesses, they try to dabble their hands into too many things all at once without specializing or getting a breakthrough in any. The result is regret, envy, resentment, and bitterness that their efforts are not yielding fruits. They fail to realize that they have become Jacks of all trades who are masters of none.

Before you decide whether you want to run multiple businesses or not, you need to remember that owning a business is different from running a business. Rich people may own multiple businesses, but they always run one at a time. Owning a business means hiring staff to execute the daily operations of

"Billionaires own multiple businesses. However, they focus on one business and make sure it has grown before they use it as a base for going into other businesses."

businesses without being unnecessarily agitated or concerned about what is going on in the company. But running a business means playing the leading role in providing specific directions about the daily operations of the business. In most of the multiple companies that billionaires own, they have nothing to do with their daily operations because they have put a system of checks and balance in place that makes such businesses to succeed without their constant monitoring and supervision.

CHAPTER SUMMARY

- Billionaires are never afraid to try new things, but they do so with caution and care.
- A niche is 'that place where you proved your credibility and competence, garnering people's trust.' After you've gained that reputation, you just go on riding on it into any other sector or business.
- It is only after becoming a brand and building a certain level of wealth that billionaires diversify and start other businesses.
- If you rush into too many businesses too soon without being known for anything, people are likely to perceive you as someone who lacks focus or is too ambitious.
- Before you decide whether you want to run multiple businesses or not, you need to remember that owning a business is different from running a business.

PART ELEVEN

TIME CODE

One thing billionaires never allow anyone to steal from them is their time. Because they are always preoccupied with many goals, time is their most cherished possession. To maximize the use of time to create massive results, billionaires use other people's time.

The time code is different from the concept of time management. Of course, billionaires have great time management skills, but their massive success is not always the result of time management alone. It is mostly the result of paying other people for their time. When a billionaire knows that there is something valuable he can get from you to increase the effectiveness of his business, he will not hesitate to pay you a reasonable amount of money to provide such service to him. Chapter 17 shows that billionaires spend their time productively.

CHAPTER 17

SKILLFUL PRODUCTIVITY

"Until your busyness becomes commensurate with your income, you are said to be unproductive and unskillful in your business."
– Dr Stephen Akintayo

To reach billionaire status, you must be skillful in your productivity. In other words, you must be willing to prioritize productivity over activity. Hence, billionaires hate activity but love productivity. But poor people are always actively unproductive. They are always busy achieving

"Untill your busyness becomes commensurate with your income, you atr said to be unproductive and unskillful in your business"

little or nothing at all. In a paradoxical fashion, poor people seem to be busier while their businesses seem to be bringing little or no profit.

Someone once made a statement that made me think. He said, "To be busy is to be under Satan's yoke." While this may sound like pontification, the fact is that there are many people who are always busy but producing little or no result. Until your busyness becomes commensurate with your income, you are said to be unproductive and unskillful in your business.

Billionaires prioritize productivity over activity. Productivity deals with the measurement of effectiveness while activity deals with the measure of movement. Meaningful activity can lead to productivity, but it is not the case that productivity often results from too much activity. You can be unproductively active when the activities you are engaged in are not producing positive or profiting results.

> *"To be productive, you must learn to sharpen your skills. A skill is a field of expertise that enables you to do something more efficiently and productively."*

Poor people prioritize activity over productivity. They are always occupied with many things, which do not produce anything substantial for them. They love to jump from one activity to another and move from one place to another. They think that by so much movement and actions they are productive. But at the end of such busyness, they can hardly point to something meaningful they have been able to achieve during the day. Most poor people erroneously presume that activity determines productivity. So, they try to accomplish so much in a little time and end up producing the opposite effect of doing so little with so much time.

Prioritize Productive Activity

To be productive, you must learn to sharpen your skills. A skill is a field of expertise that enables you to do something more efficiently and productively. Having many skills is an advantage when it comes to business and entrepreneurship. The more skillful you are, the more likely you are to be productive and succeed in your business.

Many poor people are unproductive because they have not grasped the concept of prioritization. Working without priorities is like shooting without aim. You cannot become skillfully productive if you do not put certain standards in place to help you prioritize your activities and daily engagements. You must endeavor to strategize on how to be more productive than just filling your day with many activities. Remember that having so much work to do is not the same as accomplishing much. You can be busy doing so much within the day but end up achieving just a little.

> *"To escape the pitfall of unproductivity, you must be determined to prioritize your work and time based on their importance. That is, commit your time to work that helps you get the most productive results."*

To escape the pitfall of unproductivity, you must be determined to prioritize your work and time based on their importance. That is, commit your time to work that helps you get the most productive results. Remember, it is possible to be overloaded with unproductive work.

Practice Time Management

The ability to manage your time is a key determinant of your productivity and success. Many people are unproductive because they have not mastered the art of time management. They allow many distractions to impede their routines thereby capitulating their effectiveness and productivity. At the time when they are supposed to be more productive, they find themselves trying to attend to unnecessary and unimportant demands.

For example, many poor people are in the habit of checking their emails and social media several times within working hours. Some people even start their day by checking their phones.

"In a somewhat ironic manner, the technologies that are meant to enhance our productivity have become our major impediments to productivity.

Several studies have shown the devastating impact that electronics such as phones have on general productivity. In a somewhat ironic manner, the technologies that are meant to enhance our productivity have become our major impediments to productivity.

Here is a key principle to work with that will help you manage your time more effectively and avoid unnecessary distractions—Disciplined planning. Billionaires detest unplanned and random activities. Because they work based on schedule, they have each day well-planned ahead of time that they do not allow emergencies to distract or interrupt those plans. They have trained

"Over the years, through discipline and dedication, I have trained myself to be accountable about how I spend my time each day. In other words, I have learned to be productive with my time."

themselves to be disciplined in managing their time that people who lack such discipline may sometimes regard them as cold-headed and nonchalant.

Most poor people think that because they waste time chasing shadows, they can waste other people's time too in such vain pursuits. Sometimes, people excitedly say things to me as, "I want to come to your office."; "I want to see you."; "I want the two of us to spend some time together." But when I ask what they want to achieve by such meetings, they get offended. They feel like I do not cherish our friendship or whatever it is that we share. They do not recognize that I don't waste time doing things that do not add up to my productivity.

Over the years, through discipline and dedication, I have trained myself to be accountable about how I spend my time each day. In other words, I have learned to be productive with my time. If I have been careless with how I spend my time, I would not have made enough money for such people to want to meet up with me. I always think of the time I spend with people in terms of value. And that is one of the secrets of billionaires. They are always asking: How productive have I been spending my time? What value do my various meetings add to me and my business? These are key principles of time management that every serious-minded person who wants to be productive in business must practice. Time management is a great principle that every billionaire has learned to pay attention to.

"Make sure that your life philosophy is focused on what can bring results. Remember, result terminates insult."

Focus on Results

Wealth is a result of productivity, not activity. If you want to generate wealth, therefore, you must learn to focus your energy and attention on doing things that bring results rather than engaging in aimless and goalless activities. Billionaires are rewarded for the results they have generated and not the time they have spent. The moment you start focusing on results and not activity, you will start noticing a change in your productivity and bank account. This is because it is results that make one wealthy, not the many things that he or she does. Make sure that your life philosophy is focused on what can bring results. Remember, result terminates insult.

Many times, people contact me that they want to have a meeting with me. But after directing them to schedule a time for such meetings with my secretary, I usually see the disappointment on their face or notice it in the tone of their voice. But the truth is that for me to continue to be effective, I must work based on a schedule. I cannot afford to have unplanned meetings with my friends, relations, and family members who may end up taking most of my time just talking about things that do not have any direct bearing on my business and productivity. Before I meet with you, I must first ascertain: What is the *telos* of the planned meeting? How is this meeting going to enhance my productivity? How is our meeting going to be mutually beneficial?

Because most poor people do not understand the principle of focusing on results, when they start a business or join a company, they often assume that by mere coming early to work and closing late they are productive. For those who work for others, the assumption is that mere punctuality is enough to grant them promotion. In our company, we don't promote people because of their punctuality. We promote them based on their productivity and results. This does not mean that we are not strict on punctuality. We emphasize punctuality but place productivity above it. If you spend five hours in the office, we are more concerned about the results you have produced within those hours than we are concerned about your presence in the office.

One of the powerful contributions you can give to any organization is to focus on results. If you can help your organization to either make more money or save money, you are considered a great asset to the organization. No CEO would want to let go of such staff. This is because when you help your organization to either save or make more money, you are building the brand equity of that organization. Contribute toward making your company grow its brand equity or have a better name, then you have earned the right of becoming a great asset to your company. But in situations where you are punctual in reporting to work without improving the results of the business, you become a liability to the organization. Anytime you are not found to be adding tangible value, you are almost on your way out. No responsible manager or supervisor will want to promote such an employee.

"In our company, we don't promote people because of their punctuality. We promote them based on their productivity and results."

Poor people are paid for their time, but billionaires are paid for their value, productivity, and results. Have you ever wondered why billionaires are never paid per hour? Think about billionaires like Elon Musk, Bill Gates, Jeff Bezos, Warren Buffett, Aliko Dangote, Jack Ma, and Oprah Winfrey. Can you imagine what it would be like to pay these people per hour? The amount will be stupendously ridiculous. This is the reason no one talks about paying billionaires per hour. Instead, they are paid based on the value they bring to the marketplace. They are paid based on the results they have taken several years to generate. For most billionaires, it took them about ten years or more to build wealth and create the results they are currently paid for. Think about Amazon, Microsoft, Ali Baba, Dangote companies, and

"Poor people are paid for their time, but billionaires are paid for their value, productivity, and results."

many of such billion-dollar brands. How long did it take them to make such a name for themselves? This is a key principle about wealth generation that many poor people don't understand. Building a billion-dollar brand takes an awfully long time. But the good thing about such brands is that once they reach such a world-class status, they are likely to remain there for generations.

CHAPTER SUMMARY

- To reach billionaire status, you must be skillful in your productivity. In other words, you must be willing to prioritize productivity over activity.
- Until your busyness becomes commensurate with your income, you are said to be unproductive and unskillful in your business.
- To be productive, you must learn to sharpen your skills. A skill is a field of expertise that enables you to do something more efficiently and productively.
- Billionaires are rewarded for the results they have generated and not the time they have spent.
- Poor people are paid for their time, but billionaires are paid for their value, productivity, and results.

PART TWELVE

MONEY CODE

Money plays a significant role in the success of any venture. Why do we even refer to some people as billionaires if not because of the estimated value of their money? But billionaires do not pursue money as an end. They only use money to achieve their goals. They recognize the fact that money is a powerful instrument that can be used to accomplish a lot of good. So, while what drives them may not be money, they are cognizant that nothing can be achieved without it. Billionaires leverage on money to carry out their vision and execute their goals and also use money as a catalyst for growth and influence. Thus they put systems in place to continuously earn money.

Such systems are covered under the two chapters in this section. Chapter 18 brings to light the idea of *Monetized Pleasure*, which is a way billionaires keep making money even while they play. And chapter 19 explains the simple but often misunderstood concept of *Passive Income*. This is a way to make money while at rest. The Money Code lays out the fact that whether billionaires are working, resting or playing, they have active income streams.

CHAPTER 18

MONETIZED PLEASURE

"Billionaires monetize the very things they enjoy."

– Dr Stephen Akintayo

M any poor people envy, resent, judge, and castigate billionaires because they see these billionaires as people who have a lot of money and do nothing with it other than waste it in pursuit of fleeting pleasures. Little do these people know that hardly do billionaires pursue

"billionaires have learned to monetize their pleasure. They think of pleasure as an investment."

pleasure for pleasure's sake alone. Most billionaires pursue pleasure as a means to an end. In other words, billionaires have learned to monetize their pleasure. They think of pleasure as an investment.

Without a doubt, billionaires love to have fun. Some love to party and others love to travel and enjoy all the good things that life has to offer. But they do not pursue pleasure purposelessly. They always find a way to monetize their pleasures. If they love to travel, they start a tourism company or find some way to monetize their traveling. For example, one of the things I did when I started traveling was organizing seminars across the world. When I visited Italy, I organized and conducted a seminar which many people paid to attend, and in the process bought many copies of my books. In the end, the money I earned from the seminars was more than the money I spent traveling to Italy for pleasure. You can call this using one stone to kill two birds—or many birds!

". In the end, billionaires derive pleasure from their possessions, and at the same time, use them as major sources of income multiplication."

I learned the principle of monetized pleasure from Al Waleed bin Talal bin Abdulaziz Al Saud, the Saudi Arabian businessman, investor, philanthropist, and member of the Saudi royal family. He is one of the well-known billionaires in the world. He was listed as *Time Magazine's 100 Most Influential People in the World* in 2008. Al Waleed has a yacht and a private jet, and monetizes both! While outwardly many people may see him as a billionaire who wastes his resources in the purchase of expensive things, the reality is that he is thinking like a business man. He knows that his property will eventually bring him huge returns, much more than what he has invested. Many billionaires who have Rolls Royce rent them out as an additional stream of income. The same thing applies to most owners of Ferrari. They rent them out. They find a way to monetize the things that give them pleasure. In the end, billionaires derive pleasure from their possessions, and at the same time, use them as major sources of income multiplication.

> *"You don't have to have plenty of money before you start thinking of your pleasure in a way that will both give you satisfaction and benefit you."*

Another way billionaires monetize their pleasures is by registering to become members of certain clubs. For example, members of Rolls Royce Clubs form business alliances that expand their network of influence, thus exposing one another to many business ventures. If you don't know these things you'll probably keep analyzing, criticizing, and judging rich people what you perceive as a purposeless pursuit of lavish lifestyles at the detriment of the poor.

Monetize Your Pleasure

Anyone can think like a billionaire when it comes to pleasure. You don't have to have plenty of money before you start thinking of your pleasure in a way that will both give you satisfaction and benefit you. On what do you spend most of your money? What does pleasure mean to you? Is there a way you could monetize the thing that is pleasurable to you?

Many poor people spend a lot of money buying expensive phones that they end up spending a lot of money to maintain. In the end, the phones become a liability that

"The problem that many poor people have is that they tend to pursue pleasure as a telos."

usurps money from them with nothing in return. But imagine such people start thinking of how to monetize their phones, for instance, by using the phone to record comedy or educational skits to share on social media such as Facebook or YouTube. It would be incredibly astonishing how that simple change of mentality can open them up for bigger and unimaginable opportunities.

The pursuit of pleasure *and* business are not necessarily mutually exclusive when you start thinking like a billionaire: how do I monetize this thing? The problem that many poor people have is that they tend to pursue pleasure as a telos. When you make pleasure your ultimate goal in life, you will hardly make a fortune. But if you reverse that kind of thinking and begin to also see pleasure as a means of expansion, then you're on for income multiplication.

Think Long-Term

As you think about pleasure, think long-term. Don't be like the hedonists and epicureans who pursue pleasure as an end in itself. The philosophical school founded in Athens by Epicurus, which came to be known as Epicureanism, maintained that the pursuit of pleasure is the highest good in life. Although the epicureans regarded mental pleasure (freedom from anxiety and fear) more highly than physical pleasure,

"Don't be like the hedonists and epicureans who pursue pleasure as an end in itself."

it was this philosophy that later gave birth to hedonism. The hedonists think that the pursuit of pleasure is the most important thing in life. Therefore, they can do anything to achieve that objective. When the pursuit of pleasure becomes the major objective in life, many problems are bound to surface. The hedonists don't think about the implications of their pursuits in so far as they get what they want in the process. They are the ones who can do anything for pleasure's sake.

Most billionaires will not subscribe to either epicurean or hedonistic ideologies. They think about pleasure based on its long-term implications. For instance: would my pursuit of pleasure cost me a fortune? How would this affect my business reputation?

"Wouldn't it be nice if everyone decided to face their lives and become wealthy instead of paying unnecessary attention to other people's lifestyles?"

Would this have dire financial consequences? Is this move going to greatly impact my income negatively? These are some of the questions that billionaires ask before they pursue any kind of pleasure. If after their analysis and consultations they realize that their pursuit will impact them negatively, many will choose to forego the pleasure. Not so with poor people. Most poor people pursue pleasure based on instincts and emotions. This explains why they have continued to remain poor. To break such a habit, you must learn to monetize your pleasure.

And no, you don't pursue the pleasure you cannot yet comfortably afford as a means of keeping up with the Rich Family down the road. Billionaires don't waste their time being unnecessarily concerned or agitated about other people's lifestyles; monitoring the various things other people engage in; or what others consider pleasurable. They have a lot before them and hardly enough hours to get down to action. But that is exactly the problem of most poor people—too much time spent doing what doesn't count.

Most poor people make it a habit to monitor rich people's lifestyles so they can find something to criticize. Rather than facing their lives, they face other people's

"Most poor people pursue pleasure based on instincts and emotions."

lives and become embittered by the various experiences that others seem to be having that they can't. Wouldn't it be nice if everyone decided to face their lives and become wealthy instead of paying unnecessary attention to other people's lifestyles?

Billionaires don't pursue pleasure for pleasure's sake alone but monetize the very things they enjoy. That's a code to wealth multiplication. Earn while you play!

CHAPTER SUMMARY

- Billionaires have learned to monetize their pleasure. They think of pleasure as an investment.
- In the end, billionaires derive pleasure from their possessions, and at the same time, use them as major sources of income multiplication.
- You don't have to have plenty of money before you start thinking of your pleasure in a way that will both give you satisfaction and benefit you.
- Billionaires think about pleasure based on its long-term implications.
- And billionaires don't pursue the pleasure outside their finanacial reach.

CHAPTER 19

PASSIVE INCOME

"If you have to 'work' for every money you earn, where then is financial freedom?"
– Dr Stephen Akintayo

Billionaires create systems that continuously generate money for them without the need to constantly monitor or get actively involved in the process. Such income is technically known as passive income. Specifically, passive income is

"Specifically, passive income is the money earned automatically with little or no effort on the part of the earner."

the money earned automatically with little or no effort on the part of the earner.

The nomenclature "passive" can be misleading. Many people hear the words *passive income* and immediately think of someone earning money that he or she does not deserve. They think of using magic formulas like affirmations and voodoo to generate continuous income that they have not worked for. But in reality, passive income is not *really* passive. It demands action on the part of the earner, at least at the beginning when one works hard to set up such a reliable system of money generation. It only becomes passive after one has laboriously put a working system in place that continues to generate income constantly and automatically. A few examples of passive income ideas will help explain what the concept means.

It is not news that many billionaires make a lot of money from real estate. In other words, they purchase property and rent them out, thus making these rents their major source of passive income. Rental activities are a sure way for creating passive income. Most landlords receive monthly income from their rental property on a consistent basis without having to interact with their tenants or do anything specifically. Because they have already purchased the property and put a system in place that continues to generate money for them, they are confident of receiving certain amounts of money on monthly or annual basis from their tenants. They usually do not need to do anything other than get paid!

The same thing goes for authors. Writing a book can be tasking, but when a book is published and begins to generate income, there is no limit to how much income the author will continue to get from the sale of the book. Book sales income can outlive the author and in some cases, last for centuries, depending on the success and relevance of the book. One successful book is enough to change a person's financial posterity. In this sense, a successfully published book can be said to be a source of passive income for the author.

Create a System

At the beginning of their career, billionaires work hard almost on daily basis for several years until they have a strong financial base and a system for generating passive income. After that, they leverage their hard work by creating many more passive income generation systems while they find time to rest, have fun, and enjoy the benefits of their investments. These systems range from real estate to different kinds of investments and businesses.

Two important statements about passive income have been credited to Warren Buffett. On one occasion he is quoted to have said, "You can never be rich until you make money while you sleep." On another occasion, Buffett said, "If you don't find a way to make money while you sleep, you will work until you die." The two statements are closely related. On one hand, Buffett shows the importance of creating a system that will keep generating money without you having to do anything or do so much in the process. On the other hand, he points to the danger of continuously toiling for income that is

"People who think that the only way to earn money is by working continuously for it are likely to remain poor."

characteristic of billions of people in the world. People who think that the only way to earn money is by working continuously for it are likely to remain poor. Such people work with the erroneous mentality that money must be earned through daily toil.

"Billionaires are always thinking outside the box. They are mostly unconventional in the way they approach business."

They fail to realize that such a work mentality does not make people rich. People who build wealth are those who have put certain systems in place that continue to generate money for them while they are asleep. This is a crucial part of the money-generating code.

Apply Wisdom

To create a system that generates passive income, you must apply wisdom in your work from day one. Remember, passive income does not just happen; it is created. It is wisdom when you concentrate your energy and attention on building certain structures and systems that will generate money for you while you sleep. For instance, you can create online courses or videos, write a book, run a blog, start a dropshipping store, create an app, invest in stocks, do affiliate marketing, and several other creative ideas. It is all about applying wisdom from where you are, at the very point you're at, to get what you want.

Think outside the box. The *box* is so large and full of so many people that the few who think outside it are the ones that become wealthy and free. Billionaires are always thinking outside the box. They are mostly unconventional in the way they approach business. That is a quality of people who create systems that bring them passive income. But many people prefer to have "secured" jobs that give them a guarantee of such

". Remember, passive income does not just happen; it is created."

things as monthly salary, job security, health insurance, and retirement benefits. They abhor going against anything that appears to be unconventional. As such, the idea of passive income often seems strange to them. Such people do not know how to automate. They are always working hard but not smart. It's as if they have willfully surrendered their will to the control of another person or organization. They fail to realize that through the application of wisdom they can create systems that work best for them and bring them guaranteed income while they sleep and enjoy what they have.

The irony of having "conventional" jobs is that one may continue to work until retirement without having time to enjoy the fruit of his work. At best, he realizes that all his work

"The way to know that you have attained the status of financial freedom and independence is to scrutinize your income-generating systems."

is geared toward paying bills. But not so with people who have a billionaire mindset. For such people, rather than work to pay bills, they put little or no effort and continue to be paid for the services that their systems provide to others.

You can never be financially independent until you are able to put a system in place that generates money for you while you sleep. If you have to work for every money you earn, and when you stop working money stops flowing in, you'll be tied down to that work for as long as there're bills to pay. Where then is financial freedom? The way to know that you have attained the status of financial freedom and independence is to scrutinize your income-generating systems. What brings you money? How often do you receive such income? Can anything happen overnight that will threaten the flow of that income? Do you have to

> *"Wise people create a system and build a structure that guarantees the flow of income into their bank accounts without having to worry about most of life's contingencies that millions of people—who are yet to be financially free—must worry over."*

work hard to earn that income? Can you decide to go on a vacation anytime you want without feeling guilty about skipping work? Do other people pay you anonymously?

Real estate is one of the major secrets of billionaires' passive income. Hardly would you find a billionaire who does not have real estate that generates passive income for him or her. It is the easiest way toward financial freedom. One of our customers bought one of our estates in Lagos, Nigeria. When she came to our office again, she was smiling. When I asked the cause of such happiness, she reported that she had just sold the property she bought from us three years earlier and gained a six million naira profit from it. She bought the property from us at the cost of two million naira. Can you imagine the feeling of gaining such a profit within such a short time? She later told me that she had specifically come to the office to show her appreciation to our company. This is how people become billionaires. Wise people create a system and build a structure that guarantees the flow of income into their bank accounts without having to worry about most of life's contingencies that millions of people—who are yet to be financially free—must worry over.

CHAPTER SUMMARY

- Passive income is the money earned automatically with little or no effort on the part of the earner.
- Rental activities are a sure way for creating passive income.
- At the beginning of their career, billionaires work hard almost on daily basis for several years until they have a strong financial base and a system for generating passive income.
- You don't have to actively put in time and energy for every money you earn. An established system can generate income for you.
- The way to know that you have attained the status of financial freedom and independence is to scrutinize your income-generating systems.

PART THIRTEEN

GIVING CODE

Billionaires do not give their time and resources to others aimlessly and purposelessly. They practice purposeful and targeted giving. Giving, for them, serves to open many doors of opportunity, connection, expansion, and growth.

The fact is that billionaires give more to get more. And this code is always working for them. They contribute millions of dollars in acts of charity, philanthropy, and humanitarian services each year and gain double returns of what they have given away. If you want to find out how specifically they do this, Chapter 20 reveals a worthy principle.

BENEVOLENCE PRINCIPLE

"You cannot be a true giver and not get back in multiple returns. If you want an easy and faster route to multiplying your income and wealth, try giving."

– Dr. Stephen Akintayo

Giving is a universal principle that guarantees success and the multiplication of one's fortunes. This can be referred to as the benevolence principle. Billionaires understand this principle and therefore engage in many forms of charity and philanthropy. They know that the increase of their wealth depends to a reasonable extent on their giving.

Let me share a powerful anecdote to expatiate this claim. It is about how I got my first substantial financial breakthrough. Six years ago, the church I attended organized a 21-day prayer and fasting at the beginning of the New Year and I joyfully participated in the program. After the period of prayer and fasting, our pastor told us that he felt led to ask us to empty the money in our bank accounts and send it to the founder of our church. He said he believed that some of us who were willing to obey this injunction wasgoing to experience some unique breakthroughs. But he did not provide any information beyond that.

Now, let's face it: From a natural and logical standpoint, such an injunction does not make sense. How can you ask people to take everything they have and send it to someone who already has a good life? But guess what? For some reasons that were only to be understood in hindsight, I was "foolish" enough to obey the instruction. I went ahead and cashed out the twenty-five-thousand-naira that was in my account—which was all I had at the time—and put it in the offering. That was on a Sunday morning. This was when I was still struggling to build my bulk SMS company.

But something strange and miraculous happened the following day. On that Monday morning, I received a call from a company that wanted me to supply bulk SMS to them to the tune of thirty million naira. To say that I was astounded and at the same time perplexed would be an understatement. I thought that someone was playing a prank on me. To compound the situation, the voice on the phone sounded like that of a child. But because I had learned never to despise anyone, I consented to the request, went ahead and sent an invoice to the company.

Prior to that time, the highest business order I had ever received was for two million naira. But all of a sudden, here was I sending an invoice for thirty million naira. By Tuesday morning, I got a call from the company to inform me they were ready to pay the money into my bank account. And shortly after that call, I received an alert from my bank of their deposit of the said amount. But because my bank had never seen such a transaction in the history of my account, they had to freeze my account and interrogate me to be sure. In the end, they were convinced to allow me to use the money for my business purposes.

"Because of their benevolence, billionaires are always ahead of the people they help."

You will agree with me that anyone who receives such an abundance of money overnight and fails to see it as a breakthrough that is meant to change his financial destiny must be a foolish person. In short, that was my major financial breakthrough in life. From that point, my life and business changed for good. Isn't it amazing how a single incident can change a person's life forever?

But why did I recount this somewhat personal religious experience? It is not to try to convert anyone to my church or to make any statement about Christianity specifically. This anecdote is meant to make the case that giving is a universal principle that always works under every circumstance when it is used appropriately. And this is one of the ways billionaires multiply their money. Billionaires become richer by giving.

Give to Lead

The late M. K. O. Abiola, a former Nigerian business magnate, and politician, once illustrated that "The giving hand is always on top." By that, he meant that the benevolent person will always be ahead of those who do not give because

"Billionaires become richer by giving."

as a result of his giving, the laws of the universe work to see that he stays atop to continue to give those who are below. This is one of the powerful principles that billionaires use to continue to become richer and multiply their wealth. Because of their benevolence, billionaires are always ahead of the people they help.

The African Union recently gave Tony Elumelu a diplomatic passport that allows him to visit all parts of Africa without a visa. In fact, there is a Caribbean Island that also gave him the same traveling privileges. The question is, how did Elumelu earn those privileges while many other billionaires in Africa who are much richer than him have not been given those privileges? The answer is obvious: It is because of his many benevolent acts. The Tony Elumelu Foundation is involved in many acts of charity across the African continent. The African Union (AU), knowing the impact that the Tony Elumelu Foundation has been making on the continent, decided to grant him a diplomatic passport so that he can continue to travel freely in all parts of Africa without any restrictions. The AU sees Elumelu as a true African representative because of his Foundation's divergent acts of benevolence and philanthropy. It is not surprising that Elumelu hosts webinars for Heads of States in Africa because of the respect and trust they have for him. These are some of the advantages of benevolence.

Benevolence does not only open you up to the world, it also enhances and multiplies your influence and resources. In technical terms, this is referred to as having social capital. Social capital means "the networks of relationships among people who live and work in a particular society, enabling that society to function effectively." It follows that the one who is rich in benevolence is also rich in social capital.

Giving helps you to gain social capital, and social capital opens you up to the world. It builds strong networks of relationships that give you easy access to prominent and influential people. Because ofthe philanthropic gestures of Elumelu, Presidents of African countries beg him to come to their countries and improve the lives of their people through the various initiatives of his Foundation. Where others have to go through a lot of protocols to get to, Elumelu has easy access because of his strong social capital base.

Give to Gain

As the saying goes: Givers never lack. This is a summary of a practical universal principle that is always at work. Adam M. Grant, an American psychologist, and professor of organizational managem ent at the prestigio us Wharton Business School of the University of Pennsylvania has carried out extensive research in the area of giving and receiving. In his bestselling book, *Give and Take: A Revolutionary Approach to Success*, Grant shows that "added to hard work, talent, and luck, highly successful people need the ability to connect with others."

"Benevolence does not only open you up to the world, it also enhances and multiplies your influence and resources."

The book also explains that "givers give more than they get, takers get more than they give, and matchers aim to give and get equally; all can succeed." But the major contribution of the book is its assertion that "generous people do better at work than selfish ones." Contrary to widely held opinions, Grant demonstrates that people who are generous and kind toward others finish first.

Billionaires get richer by giving. Some people think that most billionaires give because they are nice people. The truth is that they give from the perspective of expanding their social capital in the world which in turn helps to expand their businesses and multiply their income. Such acts of philanthropy and benevolence may even serve as a way to make their businesses grow faster.

There are people who have told me over the years that the reason they decided to buy from my real estate company was that they recognized that I have a Foundation and do a lot of charity. For instance, the Stephen Akintayo Foundation pays tuition fees for orphans and helps people who have been displaced by ethno-religious crises and forced to live in Internally Diaplaced Persons' (IDP) camps. Because people see and know about the charity, benevolence, and philanthropy of my Foundation, they know that if they buy from my company, some part of the money will go into the Foundation and help those in need. In doing so, they also feel that they are indirectly contributing to helping others by merely buying from my company. I am always moved to hear such submissions from some of our customers.

Giving is one of the ways billionaires get richer. A lot of times when people tell me that rich people don't give, I just laugh. I laugh because such people do not understand that giving is actually one of the things that make billionaires richer. Have you ever wondered why many celebrities, famous people, and billionaires are always involved in one form of philanthropy or another? It is because such acts showcase them to the world as good and kind people and invariably help to open more doors and opportunities for them.

Some billionaires prefer to give privately while others do it publicly. But it doesn't matter whether the giving is done in private or in public. People get to hear about it. As a matter of fact, most billionaires have annual budgets for charity and philanthropy. They do so because of the understanding that giving brings multiple gains. You cannot be a true giver and not get back in multiple returns. If you want an easy and faster route to multiplying your income and wealth, try giving.

Give to Live

Giving is living. The benevolent individual understands the principles of a happy and fulfilling life. Giving is a powerful instrument that has been shown to increase self-esteem and life expectancy.

There are three levels of giving you must pay attention to. The first level is giving to your parents. I have just completed the construction of a house for my father. While it is a small house, at least my father is proud that his son built him a house. Although I cannot recall my father ever paying my tuition (my mother was the one who worked hard to pay our school fees!), he nevertheless played his part well in providing moral and spiritual training that has helped me to be where I am today, and I am forever grateful for that. Whether he financially took care of me or not is not the most important thing. I appreciate the fact that he was always there for me. Because he is

> *"Giving is living."*

> *"You cannot be a true giver and not get back in multiple returns. If you want an easy and faster route to multiplying your income and wealth, try giving."*

my father, he deserves my respect and gratitude. And the way to show him gratitude is to take care of his basic needs. Therefore, every month I send him some money to take care of himself.

I knew and understood the importance of taking care of my parents even before I became rich. Before my mother died, I did not have much, but I tried to help her from the little business I did while on the university campus. I remember once buying her a wristwatch after doing a trade fair which happened to be the first business that I was ever engaged in. After that business, I thought that because my mother sacrificed so much for us, it was ideal to buy her something as a token of appreciation. That act, to date, remains one of the things I did that I am so proud of. Little did I know that she was not going to live long. My mother was my heroine; she was my breadwinner. But she died young. She died while still paying my university tuition. The little I was able to do for her before her demise still brings me joy today even though she did not live long to benefit from my financial prosperity.

I think this is a good point to stress that it is only as you are faithful in little that much more can be committed into your care. It is easy for you to assume that you will give more when you have more, however, the reality is that you won't have more if you don't learn to give from the little you have. Everyone has something to give no matter how little. The billionaires that you see giving today did not wait until they had much to give before they started giving. They gave their way into more. After my mother's death, I decided to adopt two women, to whom I am not related, as my mothers. I did that because I respect them, and I look up to them to fill that vacuum in my life. For my adopted mothers, I do send them some money every month to help with their upkeep. The financial support I give them may not be something big, but it is important because they have always been there for me.

Sometimes people misunderstand the purpose of giving. They think of giving in terms of the volume of what is given not in terms of the motive. But giving is not so much about the volume as it is about the goal. It does not matter how much you have; you can decide to be sending your parents something consistently every month.

> *"There is something magical about giving to parents: It expands and increases you beyond measure because of the parental blessings that will keep pouring on you."*

There is something magical about giving to parents: It expands and increases you beyond measure because of the parental blessings that will keep pouring on you. Give to your parents and see how your life will drastically change for the better. It is not about volume. Just make sure that you send them something consistently, no matter how small. Such sacrifices toward one's parents pay off.

But a word of caution is important here: Do not sacrifice all your fortune in trying to help your parents. This is the other side of the coin that can cripple you financially. Make sure that you help your parents. But do not succumb to unreasonable financial demands from them that can cripple you. My father once wanted to trick me through indirect emotional blackmail. He would tell me, "Son, people see you on social media and keep mocking me that my son is prospering while I am suffering. They think that the life you display on social media does not reflect the kind of life your father lives." I had to frankly confront my father about such an attitude. The point is that you must be determined not to allow anyone trick you into spending all your savings on your parents. You must be discreet and moderate about it so that you will be able to grow and help them better in the future. If I had listened to my father's complaints and spent all my savings in helping him, I would not have grown financially to be able to build a house for him later.

The second level of giving is to spiritual parents or mentors. If you are a religious person and have people who are your pastors or imams or the leaders of any religion that you practice, you must learn to give to support such people because of their spiritual oversight over you. They pray for you and work hard to provide spiritual nourishment to you. Some of them do not only pray for you but they also fast for you. That is why it is important to make sure that you set aside something to support your spiritual mentors because of the spiritual covering they provide over your life. Some spiritual atmospheres can either take you up or bring you down. If someone plays an important role in helping you spiritually, it is only logical that you reciprocate by giving to that person. This is a powerful principle because the more you give them, even if they don't see you or

> *"If someone plays an important role in helping you spiritually, it is only logical that you reciprocate by giving to that person."*

talk about your specific giving, their spirit is praying for you. They constantly think about you and pray to God about your prosperity. The third level of giving is to the poor.

A lot of people in Africa erroneously think that it is only the rich who are supposed to give while the poor watch and applaud the benevolence of the rich. In fact, the person who needs to give more is the poor person because he is the one who needs more. Why do we give? Is it not to have more? Unfortunately, rich people seem to understand this principle more than poor people. While the rich keep giving and receiving great amounts in return, the poor keep being miserly with their resources and keep becoming poorer by the day.

I give more when I am broke because the whole concept of giving is to get more. For instance, why do farmers plant crops in the ground? It is because they want to have a bountiful harvest. But before they can have a bountiful harvest of the same crop, they must be willing to give some of it away. The same principle applies to giving. What does a poor person need? Money!

> *"While the rich keep giving and receiving great amounts in return, the poor keep being miserly with their resources and keep becoming poorer by the day."*

But in order to have money, he must first be willing to give out of the little he has. This does not sound logical, but it is nevertheless the operational principle of wealth multiplication that billionaires and rich people use to amass more wealth.

All my financial mentors are richer than me, but I am always contributing money to support their various endeavors. I do not do it for them but for me. For example, there is one of my mentors who is a leadership expert. I have devoured most of his books over the years and I can confidently say that his books are responsible for shaping my leadership skills and multiplying my income. Recently, I approached him to be a guest in one of my programs and his workers sent me a bill of fifty thousand dollars for that guest appearance. While the amount sounded outrageous at first, when I paused to think about all

"If you are poor, learn to give to people who are poorer than you."

the things I have learned from him over the years, my hesitation to pay that amount immediately vanished. Instead of comparing his financial status with mine and whining about the amount of money his company was charging me, I focused my on all the benefits I have enjoyed from his services and the multiplier effect that his presence in my program would have.

Give Your Way up

If you are poor, learn to give to people who are poorer than you. I started doing charity while I was still a student. I and my friends would go to orphanage homes and do projects for them. We were poor students when we started helping orphans and giving to the poor. My first charity project was three thousand naira. I spoke with ten of my friends and we decided to donate three thousand naira each to help people whose socio-economic conditions were worse than ours. That was how we started. But see how far I have come. I didn't get here by luck. I understood the principle of giving and decided to put it into practice.

In case you are reading this book and you really desire to become a billionaire but where you are presently financially doesn't look like things will ever change, the truth is that you can give your way up. By that I mean you can catalyze your growing up financially by giving. Yes, you can start from the little you have like I shared about myself. The truth is everyone has something to give. The question to ask is if everyone is willing to give.

You need to understand that what makes billionaires stand out essentially is their mindset. They are always thinking about how to give more. It's more about the willingness to give than the possession they have. The truth is that if you find it hard to give out of your ten dollars, you will find it hard to give out of a thousand dollars or more. It is better to learn to give from the little that you have consistently than wait until you have more to give permanently.

CHAPTER SUMMARY

- Giving is a universal principle that guarantees success and the multiplication of one's fortunes.
- Because of their benevolence, billionaires are always ahead of the people they help.
- Benevolence does not only open you up to the world, it also enhances and multiplies your influence and resources.
- Giving helps you to gain social capital, and social capital opens you up to the world.
- There are three levels of giving you must pay attention to: giving to your parents, giving to your spiritual parents or mentors, and giving to the poor.

PART FOURTEEN

PROSPERITY CODE

What makes billionaires tick? What are the secrets of their massive wealth and prosperity? What specific things are they doing that others neglect? While poor people love to beg for money, billionaires love to provide services in exchange for money. This is one of the major secrets of their prosperity.

But billionaires do not provide any kind of services in exchange for money. They make sure that the services they are providing are massive. When they start a business, they provide the best service to the greatest number of people and become known for those services more than anyone else. From Chapters 21 to 23, we will be looking into methods through which you can create and provide the best service to the greatest number of people.

CHAPTER 21

THRIVING BUSINESS ACQUISITION

"Most billionaires have mastered three skills: How to make money, how to manage money, and how to multiply money. They apply these skills in acquiring other businesses."

– Dr. Stephen Akintayo

Billionaires prefer to make money by acquiring businesses that are structurally thriving than building new ones. The reason for this preference is that most billionaires have built businesses from the ground up and they know how rigorous and taxing starting new businesses can be. Having established their breakthrough businesses, they prefer to acquire established businesses than start new ones all over again.

People who start new businesses and are willing to sell them stand to benefit from billionaires who are looking for new businesses to acquire or invest in. But billionaires do not acquire any new business just because it is new. The owners of the business must have proven their worth and scaled the business to a reasonable extent before they can attract billionaires' interest. There are hundreds of thousands of new businesses that never attract the attention of billionaires simply because the owners have not brought something unique to the marketplace to attract billionaire investors or acquirers. Sometimes the business idea may be a good one, but billionaires are not looking for just good business ideas; they are looking for good business ideas that can scale and bring them great profits upon their acquisition. Remember, billionaires have stayed so long on the business trail to know which ones can easily scale and bring profit and which ones may not.

> *"Remember, billionaires have stayed so long on the business trail to know which ones can easily scale and bring profit and which ones may not."*

> *"Billionaires prefer to make money by acquiring businesses that are structurally thriving than building new ones."*

For instance, before Mark Zuckerberg, the Founder and CEO of Facebook (now Metaverse at the time of writing this book), purchased Instagram and WhatsApp from the owners to become part of his social networking businesses, he had already spent several years as one of the early pioneers in that technological field to know the kind of social networks that were going to be successful and add more value to his already successful businesses. Also, before the owners of Google purchased YouTube, they had done a lot of feasibility research and understood the value that such a video-sharing site would add to their company. I can give several examples of the different companies that Jeff Bezos purchased to become part of Amazon over the years. This has become the trend and culture among billionaires, especially the founders and CEOs of the Great Four: Facebook, Apple, Amazon, and Google.

This is a practical example of what I plan to do in our company in the coming years. I want to start expanding our business in the technology sector. By that, I mean our company will start looking out for great startups in the tech sectors, especially applications and software developed by Africans to acquire. The reason is twofold. Firstly, I realized that a lot of the tech businesses that started in Africa have been taken over by westerners. It beats my imagination that African billionaires are not investing in our tech businesses. Secondly, at this point in my life, I do not want to start new companies from the scratch; I would rather acquire the ones that have already been developed and proven that they can scale.

Recently Paystack, a Nigerian startup company that processes payment problems for businesses in Africa was acquired for two hundred million dollars by Stripe, which is owned by non-Africans. The question is: aren't there Nigerian or African billionaires that would have acquired Paystack? African politicians and rich people prefer to invest in foreign companies than to invest in African startups to encourage innovation and entrepreneurship.

> *"What billionaires do is that after building wealth to a certain point, they stop thinking about starting new companies and start acquiring existing ones."*

This has got to stop. While Nigerians love to complain that foreigners have taken over all their businesses, it seems like most Africans prefer everything that is foreign compared to what they have. There are many talented young people in Africa that have great ideas. For Africa to thrive and meet up with the challenges of the twenty-first century, there must be a change of mentality about business, innovation, and entrepreneurship.

What billionaires do is that after building wealth to a certain point, they stop thinking about starting new companies and start acquiring existing ones. It does not even matter whether the owners of a company have shown interest that they want to sell or not. When billionaires see a business that has good prospects, they approach the owners and give them an offer for its acquisition. And most of such offers can be quite enticing and difficult to resist. While some owners may refuse an acquisition offer by billionaires—like in the case of Snapchat's refusal to accept Mark Zuckerberg's three billion acquisition offer—many usually find the temptation too strong to resist.

> *"Anyone who has ever started a business would confirm that such an enterprise requires resilience, consistency, and agility. Hence, many wouldn't want to repeat the process even if they were successful at it the first time."*

How did Bill Gates manage to become the owner of more than one hundred different companies aside from Microsoft? He certainly did not start all of them. What he did was acquire existing businesses or become one of the major stakeholders of the businesses. After spending decades building Microsoft from the ground up to become a world-class company, he could not afford to start the same kind of process all over again to build different companies. He, therefore, leveraged his billionaire status and acquired several other businesses without having to sweat for them.

Billionaires know too well that starting a business is too demanding and taxing. And because they are not willing to tread on the same route that they are acquainted with, they prefer to acquire other businesses. Anyone who has ever started a business would confirm that such an enterprise requires resilience, consistency, and agility. Hence, many wouldn't want to repeat the process even if they were successful at it the first time.

At this point in my career, I would rather acquire an existing business than start a new one. An acquisition is much simpler to do. All it takes is for me to look out for a good business that seems to be struggling to scale, make the owners an offer, acquire it if they are willing to accept my offer, then use my experience and resources to scale it. If I decide to own a radio or television station, I do not have time to start such a process from the scratch. What I would do, instead, is to acquire an existing radio or television station and use my resources to scale it. This is how billionaires think.

Business acquisition is one of the powerful secrets of billionaires. Most billionaires have mastered three skills: How to make money, how to manage money, and how to multiply money. They apply these skills in acquiring other businesses.

Angel Investors

Some billionaires, instead of acquiring new businesses may decide to become angel investors. An angel investor is someone who has strong economic capital and is willing to invest in new businesses in exchange for equity in the business or some convertible debt. Such a person is willing to take the risk of putting his capital in a great business idea with the hope that it will scale and bring profits.

Billionaires who decide to become angel investors are risk-takers. Because of the risk involved in such investments, angel investors are always looking for a higher percentage of profit and returns for their investment. They typically ask for percentages of return as high as twenty-five to sixty percent. The reason is: it is much easier to lose money by investing in new startups than in a company that has already scaled. This explains why many billionaires desist from investing as angels. But even the few that defy the odds to do it go into the process with a lot of caution.

"Most billionaires have mastered three skills: How to make money, how to manage money, and how to multiply money. They apply these skills in acquiring other businesses."

They take their time to do a lot of research about the

business idea and the owners before putting their money into it. They always want to be sure that the risk they are about to take is worth the pain.

Venture Capitalists

Billionaires who do not become angel investors sometimes may choose to act as venture capitalists. A venture capitalist is someone who invests a substantial amount of money in a business that has already accrued a significant amount of revenue. In other words, venture capitalists invest in businesses that have already scaled. Such investments are usually in millions of dollars. Venture capitalists get their returns through hedge funds or private equity whereby they receive a certain percentage as compensation from the profits that the companies they have invested in make.

One of the advantages of the venture capitalist business model is that it helps businesses to scale and provide volume. In doing so, it also establishes credibility for the company. That way, both the company and the investors end up gaining from the partnership. While the owners

> *"Billionaires who decide to become angel investors are risk-takers."*

of the company rejoice because of the company's expansion and volume, the venture capitalists also have reasons to rejoice because of the percentages of profit they gain from their investment in the company. This is one easy but smart way that billionaires multiply their wealth.

CHAPTER SUMMARY

- Billionaires prefer to make money by acquiring businesses that are structurally thriving than building new ones.
- Billionaires are not looking for just good business ideas; they are looking for good business ideas that can scale and bring them great profits upon their acquisition.
- When billionaires see a business that has good prospects, they approach the owners and give them an offer for its acquisition.
- Most billionaires have mastered three skills: How to make money, how to manage money, and how to multiply money. They apply these skills in acquiring other businesses.

CHAPTER 22

LONG-TERM INVESTMENT

"If you don't think long-term, it will be increasingly difficult for you to be wealthy."

– Dr. Stephen Akintayo

In 1997, Jeff Bezos sent his first letter to shareholders of his company. The title of the letter was, "It is All About the Long Term." In that letter, the visionary CEO of Amazon, which was barely three years in existence, encouraged the shareholders and all his staff to cultivate the attitude of thinking long-term. He told them, "We can't realize our potential as people or companies unless we plan for the long term." Today, I am sure that when those shareholders remember the full content of that communication, they cannot but be grateful that they trusted

Bezos' vision and it was worth it. Amazon is today the biggest online retail company in the world and Bezos is the world's richest man because he has always thought about business as a long-term investment. Such is the power of vision.

Billionaires think about business and investment based on long-term vision and goals. They multiply their money by making a long-term investment. This way, they are able to scale their businesses in the long run. They recognize that through patience and perseverance, long-term investments usually turn out to build massive wealth.

Think Long-Term

When Elon Musk and his business partner sold PayPal for two billion dollars, he was thinking long-term. He thought of building an electric car even without having any experience working in the automobile industry. But barely less than twenty years, he actualized his vision through Tesla, the company he founded. Such vision sounded outrageous and outlandish at the time, but it has become a reality.

As at the time Musk started Tesla or at least said he was going to start a company that would build electric cars, it didn't make sense to people. He wasn't in the automobile industry when he made that ambitious proclamation, neither did anyone see the possibility of such an ambitious goal taking place before the year 2020. But Musk did not only envisage this happening, he also believed it was going to happen and he was the one who would make it happen. He succeeded because he thought long-term and decided to invest for the long haul. He knew it was going to take a long time to have such a car, but he was ready to pay the price, and today the rest is history. Musk accomplished what he set out to do by setting a long-term goal. He was able to visualize the world he wanted to create and was disciplined to follow it through and bring it to fruition. Today, Tesla is the only car company in the world that produces cars on a prepaid basis. If you go to the Tesla showroom, you are most likely not going to see a readymade car available for purchase. When you want to buy their car, you must preorder it within a couple of months or years before it is produced for you.

"Billionaires do what their mates are not doing today so that they can afford what their mates cannot afford tomorrow."

"Billionaires think about business and investment based on long-term vision and goals."

Billionaires do what their mates are not doing today so that they can afford what their mates cannot afford tomorrow. Many people are afraid to think big—to see a vision of a fabulous future. The problem is not so much that people are not ambitious or do not have a great vision about the future. Most people assume that if they share their ambitious future goals with their friends, family members, or neighbors, they would be deemed to be insane. Therefore, they prefer to remain mute or abandon such goals altogether.

To think long-term, you must learn to think big. David J. Schwartz, the American professor and author of the bestselling book, *The Magic of Thinking Big*, explains that "Those who believe that they can move mountains, do. Those who believe they can't, cannot. Belief triggers the power to do." Schwartz went on to say, "Belief in great results is the driving force, the power behind great books, plays, scientific discoveries. Belief in success is behind every successful business, church and political organization. Belief in success is the one basic, absolutely essential ingredient of successful people."

People who think big, think long-term. Because they have a great vision of the future, they are patient to endure whatever pain the present moment may bring for the sake of attaining their long-term goals. They do not allow today's travails and predicaments to distort their vision for the future.

They think about the future that they want to create and go ahead to create it. In other words, they invest in their long-term vision.

Invest with the Future In Mind

Billionaires multiply their money by investing in the future. But many people make the mistake of saying they want to invest only in businesses that are currently thriving and bring lots of profits. Because they seek immediate profits, they fail to think and plan for the future. They think only from short-term perspectives. But billionaires think twenty, fifty, or even a hundred years ahead.

GText is currently the largest green and smart homes developer in Africa. Our vision is to become the largest green and smart homes developer in the world by year 2035 as we plan to actualize our goal of building twenty-five thousand housing units. But someone may consider my vision too grandiose and idealistic. Some may even think of it as too ambitious. They may say things like, "You know, you are currently doing well in the business arena. Why don't you just relax and take things easy?" The fact is that we have already started developing vision 2050 to be the largest organic integrated farm in Africa. Since we know that one of the biggest causes of poverty in Africa is the inability to refine and process natural resources into consumables, we are already thinking and planning toward taking this challenge head-on.

Billionaires do not think about the here and now alone; they also think long-term. Anytime I think business, I think long-term. For instance, people would take me to a land in a community that is not yet developed. Sometimes, the topography of the land may not show signs of any future business prospects or dividends. But because I am always thinking long-term, I would show an interest in purchasing the land to the amazement of many who are only thinking about the here and now. My interest to purchase the property may not make any logical sense to such people. I remember when we first bought the land for our first estate, which later came to be known as Sapphire Estate, we could not take customers there to show them the property because it was water-logged. We could only stand from a distance and point the land to them. That constituted a huge challenge for us. But I was never discouraged. Today, the

"Billionaires do not think about the here and now alone; they also think long-term."

"If you don't think long-term, it will be increasingly difficult for you to be wealthy."

story is different. The estate is now a beautiful scene to behold because of the amount of work that has gone into it over the years.

Such is the secret of wealth creation. Always think and plan long-term because that is what billionaires do. If you don't think long-term, it will be increasingly difficult for you to be wealthy. Most Africans are struggling because everyone is always thinking about short-term goals. That is why many Africans would rather join politics as a means of getting rich quickly through corrupt practices than to think long-term and create lasting wealth for their posterity. The idea of shortcuts appeals to many. They hardly realize that shortcuts often end up lengthening the journey than proper planning and patience would. Until Africans start building structural systems that allow people of all socio-economic classes in the society to be able to tap into the many resources in the continent and create wealth, they will continue to depend on the West to spoon-feed them.

Billionaires do not think, plan, and execute on a short-term basis. They are always looking and planning ahead. My plan is that before I resign from or retire from my company as its CEO, we would have thought about and written down our 2100 vision. That is what I plan to handover to my successor. This is how companies that continue to generate wealth from one generation to another are built. We are building a company that will continue long after we are gone. We are building a company that will keep thriving with its vision untainted from one generation to another.

Invest in Posterity and Legacy Projects

Billionaires multiply their wealth by investing in posterity and legacy projects. These are the kinds of projects that outlive their owners. Examples of such projects include things like establishing schools and building hospitals. I am currently working on a couple of such projects that will outlive me. For instance, I have the vision of building schools to raise future leaders. My idea is to integrate the educational subjects with teaching on entrepreneurship where every student will be required to take several classes on entrepreneurship and learn about money. Before their graduation, each student should be able to explain what money is and how to make, manage, and multiply it. It will be a mixture of traditional formal education with entrepreneurial skills. The aim is to raise the next generation of billionaires and to write my name in the sand of time.

"Billionaires multiply their wealth by investing in posterity and legacy projects. These are the kinds of projects that outlive their owners."

Richard Branson, the English billionaire, businessman, and founder of the *Virgin Group*, has been working on a project for people to go on vacation on Mars. I learned Elon Musk is also working on the same kind of vision. Right now, such a goal might appear ambitious and unrealistic, but I believe that it will happen in the near future. No one can say whether Branson or Musk will live to see its actualization but that doesn't matter. What matters is the legacy they will leave behind. By the time people start going for a vacation on Mars fifty years from now or less, Branson or Musk may not be alive, but posterity will remember them for good because of the legacy they have left behind.

We remember the Wright Brothers today for their tenacity in building the first aircraft. We remember Thomas Edison today for trying ten thousand times before he succeeded in creating the first incandescent light bulb. Many people remember John D.Rockefeller for the vision he had to transform Manhattan into one of the great cities in the world. Andrew Carnegie is remembered for leading the expansion of the American Steel Industry in the nineteenth century. J. P. Morgan is remembered for reorganizing and

"Think long-term. Think legacy. Think posterity."

modernizing the railroad systems in America and subsequently throughout the world. He is also remembered for initiating the banking revolution. Henry Ford is remembered for the introduction of the Model T automobile which revolutionized transportation and the American industry. These people have written their names in the sand of time by doing something bigger than them. Little wonder their names have continued to live long after their demise and each generation will continue to remember them for their contributions. It is not surprising that the Rockefeller Foundation and the Carnegie Foundation have continued to exist to this day. These billionaires multiplied their influence and businesses because they were thinking about posterity and legacy projects. That is why we remember them to this day.

What would you want to be remembered for in the coming generations? Think long-term. Think legacy. Think posterity.

CHAPTER SUMMARY

- Billionaires think about business and investment based on long-term vision and goals.
- Billionaires do what their mates are not doing today so that they can afford what their mates cannot afford tomorrow.
- Billionaires do not think about the here and now alone; they also think long-term.
- If you don't think long-term, it will be increasingly difficult for you to be wealthy.
- Billionaires multiply their wealth by investing in posterity and legacy projects.

DIVERSIFIED INVESTMENT

"One of the rules of investment is to never invest in any venture an amount of money that you cannot afford to lose."

– Dr. Stephen Akintayo

One of the many advantages that rich people have over poor people is in the way they diversify their investments. Most billionaires have understood the caution not to put all their eggs in one basket. But while the concept of putting one's eggs in one basket has generated a lot of controversy among investment experts in recent years, I will only highlight those controversies where necessary so that they do not distract us from the objective of this chapter.

The so-called controversy about diversified investment, or what some prefer to call multiple streams of income, is often attributed to Andrew Carnegie, the Scottish-American industrialist and businessman, who once said, "Put your eggs in one basket and watch that basket." While Carnegie's statement is often taken out of context, it has often been used to argue against the diversification of business and investment.

The concept of diversification of investment connotes the ability to understand and invest in different ventures and not allow oneself to be limited to one source of income. There are many advantages to the diversification of income. These include, but are not limited to reduction of volatility, minimization of risk, safeguard against adverse economic trends, capital security, compound interest, and security of income.

Most billionaires invest in diversified ventures. They do not limit themselves to one source of investment because they understand that doing so may constitute a lot of risk in times of economic downturns and adversity.

Understand Investment Risks

Risk entails doing something that has the potential of becoming dangerous or affecting one negatively. Every investment has a potential risk, but the degree of risk varies significantly based on the type of investment. No discussion of investment returns is practical and meaningful without an analysis of the potential risk involved. While factors that determine risk can be controversial or debatable, it is advisable that you think of risk in terms of the odds that an investment venture may fail to achieve the returns that it has promised. In other words, think of risk as the barriers that could potentially

" While factors that determine risk can be controversial or debatable, it is advisable that you think of risk in terms of the odds that an investment venture may fail to achieve the returns that it has promised."

y create losses in an investment.

Generally, investment risks could be categorized as low-risk, mid-risk, and high-risk. Low-risk investments are those which have a low stake in terms of the amount of money invested and the guarantee of returns. Mid-risk, as the name implies, is that which stands between low-risk and high-risk. Mid-risk investments may present good odds of either success or failure. But on the most part, they have a high percentage of success. High-risk investments are those which have a higher percentage of serendipity and chance. On one hand, you have a higher chance of making a great profit but on the other hand, you also have a higher chance of losing everything.

Billionaires invest in low-risk, mid-risk, and high-risk ventures. But they put most of their fortune in low risk, some of it in mid-risk, but only an insignificant portion in high-risk. That way, they are able to maintain their financial balance without the trepidation of becoming bankrupt overnight.

"But poor people only invest in high-risk ventures. This is because most poor people tend to think of investment as an opportunity to get rich quickly.

But poor people only invest in high-risk ventures. This is because most poor people tend to think of investment as an opportunity to get rich quickly. This is the reason why there is a preponderance of get-rich-quick schemes today that a lot of people are falling for, as discussed earlier in this book. They are after fast money. Rich people, on the other hand, diversify their investment by spreading it to encompass low, mid, and high-risk ventures. They understand the principle of growing long-lasting wealth—it never happens in a rush.

Not many people know that billionaires also invest in forex. When billionaires invest in forex trading or something that might be considered high-risk, they often opt for institutional investor schemes. That is, they do not invest as individuals; they trade as institutions by either investing in mutual funds or things like pension funds. Through institutional investor, they have government license under strict regulations. But an average poor man is a lone investor, which is why poor people have high chance of suffering investment losses more than rich people.

Diversify Your Investment

To drastically reduce investment risk, you must diversify your investment portfolio. Avoid putting all your eggs in one basket. This principle becomes even more important and non-negotiable if you are a high-risk investor. To reduce risk, you must learn to diversify your investment and make sure that your diversified investments have a level of stability and do not constitute high-risk to you.

But how do you know if an investment is high-risk? The simple way to know is through the returns on the investment. Once the return is extremely high, there is no doubt that you are dealing with a high-risk investment. For instance, if someone tells you he is going to give you fifteen percent returns on your investment each month, I don't care who the person is, know that such returns on investment are not common and therefore you are dealing with high-risk investments. If you are wise, you wouldn't put all your money into such kind of investment.

Because of ignorance and lack of understanding of how investment returns work, the moment poor people hear that there is an investment that gives a monthly fifteen percent returns (which qualifies as high-risk), they carry all their money, and sometimes other people's money, and put there without giving a second thought to the risk involved. Instead of contemplating about how to divide their money into three: one portion goes to low risk, another goes to mid-risk, and then they can afford to put some portion into this new venture that is high-risk, they unadvisedly put all their eggs in a basket that is porous and unlikely to contain them.

One of the rules of investment is to never invest in any venture an amount of money that you cannot afford to lose. If you think that losing a certain amount is going to destabilize you financially and emotionally, that is a good sign that you should not do it.

Withdraw the Profit

Billionaires always withdraw the profits from their high-risk investments and put them in mid-risk and low-risk ventures which have a certain level of stability and guarantee. But what many poor people do is roll it over. God saved your head, you made a profit, instead of withdrawing the profit, you allow greed to control you to the point that you end up losing both your capital and profit!

When you do high-risk investments, make sure to pull out your profit until you make back your capital. That is, what you have invested. That is how billionaires and smart people play the game of investment. This helps especially if the investment venture eventually crashes. That way, you know that at least you got back the capital you invested. If you apply this principle in your investment, it will save you from a lot of melancholy and misfortune. But if you decide to ignore it, you don't have any justification to whine, complain, or play the victim when disaster happens.

CHAPTER SUMMARY

- Most billionaires invest in diversified ventures.
- Generally, investment risks could be categorized as low-risk, mid-risk, and high-risk.
- Rich people understand the principle of growing long-lasting wealth – it never happens in a rush.
- One of the rules of investment is to never invest in any venture an amount of money that you cannot afford to lose.
- When you do a high-risk investment, make sure to pull out your profit until you make back your capital. That is, what you have invested. That is how billionaires and smart people play the game of investment.

PART FIFTEEN

LOAN CODE

Starting a business relies primarily on capital. You'll agree with me that a good business structure cannot be well put together if it is lacking in the area of finance. This crucial need has lured a lot of un-smart business owners into incurring huge debts. With the large span of easily accessible loan platforms in recent times, a lot of startups and long-existing businesses have been caught in the web of repaying loans accompanied by frightening interests, one reason why some businesses only existed for a short time and ended shutting down due to bankruptcy. Hence it has become very crucial for every business owner to explore different ways and options of coming up with needed capital by leveraging the resources that are within their reach instead of jumping on the next available loan option. That is how billion-worth empires are made and sustained.

Many great business ideas have crumbled before making it a mile ahead because they were poorly managed. Sustainability of any goal and vision comes with the constant evolution and renovation of ideas. The world's market keeps changing constantly due to the incessant change in climate, price, need, trend, demand, and many more factors. Keeping up with the pace of the alteration in these factors of sales is what business owners have failed to achieve. Taking loans to sort out every financial problem that might come up is a bad idea for any company. In the long run, it results in pile ups and renders the business handicapped and frustrated.

One of the crucial billionaire codes is to generate capital by looking inward and not outward. By this, I mean to say that capital can be strategically generated by leveraging the readily available resources or by looking into what can be done better to spur a change in the situation on ground. In Chapter 24, I talk extensively about the strategies that can help you imbibe the billionaire loan code, helping you consider taking loans only when it is advantageous and never to your detriment.

SCALED BUSINESSES

"Scaling is more than a mere growth in numbers."

– Dr. Stephen Akintayo

Scaling a business means expanding the business and taking it to the next level. The art of scaling means having the ability to grow without being hindered. It means injecting money into your business and revenue engines while making sure that you have the right people in the right places. Knowing when to scale a business is as important as the business itself. This is the ability to set the stage to enable and enhance support and growth for your business. But scaling is more than a mere growth in numbers. It means the ability to apply certain principles that will automate and generate substantial revenue for the business. It is not so much about the size of your business compared to its emphasis on the principle of expansion and sustainability.

Scaling is a process that consciously shifts the business into the limelight of big opportunities. It requires good planning, organizing, strategizing, funding, and putting the right legal and operational systems in place for effectiveness. With a focus on getting the support of investors who will be willing to put huge money into your business. As such, it also requires excellent and exceptional commitment and focus. This often requires doing something exceptionally well that puts your business ahead of the competition by running miles ahead of them. When this has been achieved, your business would grow and expand exponentially. For this to become a reality, you need to master the art of scaling.

Every successful business has a tipping point. *The Tipping Point*, according to Malcolm Gladwell in a book with the same title, "is that magic moment when an idea, trend, or social behavior crosses a threshold, tips, and spreads like wildfire." The two important things about scaling are understanding the law of timing and mastering the art of using other people's time and money. That is always the perfect time to scale every business. We can add "business" into this definition. From a business perspective, a tipping point is a place where a great idea, nurtured by a great businessman or businesswoman, utilizes great human and material resources to scale a business.

Billionaires have mastered the art of scaling. They also know when to take their business public and grow it massively. This requires that they study the times and seasons that are right for the implementation of each idea. Since scaling requires knowing the right strategy, people, and timing, billionaires do not take it lightly. They can sacrifice a lot of their comfort to see that they grow a business to a point that it will scale without any impediments.

Scaling can turn out to be the most exhilarating period of a business when approached skillfully and timely but if proper mechanics are not put in place, scaling can turn out to be disastrous. That is why it is important to master the art of scaling.

Use OPT

Scaling businesses involves the use of several resources to make them a success. One of these factors involves leveraging on Other People's Time (OPT) for maximum scaling of their business. Billionaires know and understand how to use Other People's Time (OPT). That is, they employ the services of other people who play important roles to enhance the growth of their business and grow it exponentially. The effective use of OPT is a strategy that must be embraced by anyone who wants to build a business that will grow massively and generate great wealth from it.

As a counter-measure against the fact that there is a limitation to what a man can do in spite of their skillfulness and expertise, billionaires understand the wisdom of employing the services of other people to achieve their business goals and objectives. By using OPT, they make sure that their businesses can run without them because if you'll be real here, you admit that a person can only be at a place at a time. They understand that with the right people in place, it is much easier to scale and grow a business than doing everything all alone. A Hausa (one of Nigeria's languages) adage says, "*Sarkin yawa yafi sarkin karfi.*" It means, "*A multitude of army is to be preferred than the military prowess of one warrior.*" Billionaires know that no matter how skillful and talented they may be, they cannot achieve so much alone. So, they use OPT as an important strategy for continuous expansion and scaling of their businesses.

No matter how talented, gifted, educated, hard-working, and industrious you are, there is only so much you can achieve. As one of the ancient philosophers put it in the Holy writ, "*Two are better than one; because they have a good reward for their labour. For if they fall, the one will lift up his fellow: but woe to him that is alone when he falleth; for he hath not another to help him up... And if one prevail against him, two shall withstand him; and a threefold cord is not quickly broken"* (Eccl. 4:9-12, KJV).

On the contrary, poor people are the only ones who carry out all aspects of their businesses. They have failed to realize or embrace the importance of automation in doing business. Hence, they are tangled in making their business work, doing all the menial jobs and engaging in very little brain probing activity. They have not found a way to automate, unlike billionaires who always find a way to automate. That is why they keep getting rich. You know you are on your path to creating great wealth when you begin to employ experts and skillful people in your business who understand the principles of the business and can work independently in your absence, as was discussed under the replicaion principle.

Employing the use of OPT highly characterizes my business dealing. In times when I have to travel on tour to our various offices in different counties like Dubai, the United States, or the United Kingdom, I have had to stay outside Nigeria for as long as 3 months. Now, take a deep look at how it would have been in the Nigerian offices if there weren't skilled and capable set of people to handle business to the peak in my absence. Here is a practical example of something that has come to characterize my business dealings. Because I have employed skillful and capable people to handle the various operations of my companies it continues to run smoothly and thrive from wherever I am.

The same thing applies to when I leave those countries where we have businesses. There are many people in those offices who are handling the daily operations of my businesses in our various offices outside Nigeria that even if I decide to stay in Nigeria for several months without visiting those offices, I can have good sleep because I trust my employees and partners. As I am writing this, I have spent my last three months outside Nigeria, but my staff have opened and launched new estates in Nigeria. How did they manage to do that without my presence? It is because I have trained them to be acquainted with the various operations of the company such that I don't have to always be there before something great takes place. So, while I am busy expanding our businesses in Dubai and elsewhere, my staff in Nigeria are busy opening and launching several estates in my absence. This is what the art of scaling looks like.

If you plan to build a lasting business that will scale, you must be willing to put a structure in place and employ other people's time so that the business can run smoothly and thrive without your constant involvement and monitoring. Because of the lack of such structures, most poor people who start a business easily get upset and frustrated and assume that they are not lucky. One of the major reasons is, most of the people who start such businesses often start it out of frustration with their current employers or their socio-economic condition, without taking time to put certain structures in place that will make their business most likely to thrive. That is why you keep hearing that more than ninety percent of startups always fail. If you want to save yourself the headache of starting a business that will likely fail, you must be ready, from day one, to use other people's time. Some who work for others may feel that their bosses are giving them too many jobs and may decide to abruptly resign to start their business without a basic understanding of the principles we have been espousing in this book. Unsurprising, they quickly discover that their business does not seem to be making headway and they become frustrated and despondent.

To effectively make use of OPT, you do not only need to employ the services of others, but you also need to put good structures in place that will make the people that work for you learn to work independently and only report to you occasionally. Even when such people use other people's time but fail to put a structure in place that will make their business thrive in their absence, they are bound to encounter massive failure. What often happens with people who quit their jobs to start their own business is that they end up overworking themselves and go through a whole lot of stress because they don't understand certain basic business principles. Some may notice that after some time their health begins to deteriorate because of lack of good sleep and constant anxiety. They started their business under the illusion that it was going to be a rollercoaster ride, little did they know that such ventures require having a good mental and emotional stamina and, most importantly, learning the skills of using other people's time for good productivity.

Leaving an organization without having enough understanding of what success takes to start yours abruptly is very risky. I always advise the people I coach and mentor that even if you must go and start your business, you would be wise to first try to become the best friend of your boss so you can learn how he got there. Building such a relationship with your boss will help you become equipped for the position of a leader. You want to know how successful business people think and the principles and structures they apply in their businesses so you can do it right.

Scaling your business also involves the understanding of those who you intend to work with. Everyone has a niche and weakness. As a business manager, if you have not mastered the art of studying and understanding the people in your company, you might make an error with placing them in the right place where they can function maximally. You may go ahead and employ people to work for you but if you do not understand the basic ways of using people's skills, talents, and specialties for maximum productivity, you may soon be disappointed. If you blindly employ the wrong people and put them in the wrong places, they may end up causing more havoc to your business and make it crash. Suffice it to say that employing the services of other people is not synonymous with placing the right people in the right place under the right conditions. You must learn to employ the services of reliable, trusted, proven, and skillful people that will complement your weaknesses and the ones who will be able to use their initiatives to work independently to cause speedy growth in your business. Never employ people who will constantly come back to you asking for direction about every small detail on how to run the business. Such employees will end up becoming a liability to you and not an asset. Gather assets and not liabilities. This doesn't by any means imply that it is wrong for you to hire rising talents. They need to be hired and trained to get the experience that they need to grow. Everyone deserves a chance at success but let it be that you are truly gathering talents, rising or expert.

Think Business, not Product

Starting a business always requires that there is a product to be sold, a commodity to be promoted, or a service to be advertised. However, the way that you run the business determines the fate of the products. You must know that most failed businesses didn't fail because the product was bad. They failed because a good product was managed poorly. To guarantee the success of any product, the business running skill of the manager must be subjected to incessant growth till it is ranked top-notch. When thinking about running your personal business, you need to consciously draw the margin between selling a product and running a business. I must emphasize that many times, businesses fail not because the product was bad but because the owners did not know how to operate the business. A good product in the hands of someone who does not understand business principles is as good as a failed business. Having the right product alone is not sufficient to make your business succeed. You must have the right product and understand the principles of business operation.

A product is the service(s) that you plan to bring to the marketplace while a business is how you successfully make that happen. Having a product, therefore, does not qualify as having a business. Many poor people just have a good product, not a business. You must understand that investors do not invest in products, they invest in businesses. The litmus test to ascertain whether you have a business is to ask if you can leave your business for six months and nothing will go down because you have put good operational structures in place that work well in your absence. That is when we know that you have a business.

Another Look at Smart Work

The concept discussed here has already been presented in an earlier part of this book, but will be explained more deeply. Working smart means employing catalyzed means to achieve greater results than you ordinarily would have achieved. Billionaires make sure that they put a structure in place that can run even without their presence or directions. This, however, should not be mistaken to mean that billionaires are a bunch of indolent people who are always whiling time away and enjoying themselves while other people are working for them. It is not the case of "*Monkey deh work, bamboo dey chop*" as we say in Nigeria. (That idiom literally translates as, "*A monkey works while a bamboo enjoys the benefits.* "It is often used to refer to a situation where one person works hard while another enjoys the benefits without working). That is not what we are referring to here. Billionaires always make sure they set up an operational system in their businesses that can run even if they are not there.

In the true sense of it, Billionaires work harder than most poor people. But most importantly, they work smarter than an average person in business. The difference between hard work and smart work is subtle. Hard work basically entails spending long hours at work to complete certain tasks and achieve some desired results. But the person who works hard may not necessarily see his hard work translate into concrete results. Most poor people work hard all year round, but they perpetually remain poor. This is where the idea of smart work comes in. Smart work entails the art of organizing, planning, strategizing, prioritizing, and skillfully executing a task to achieve specific goals.

If you take out time to work closely with most billionaires, you will know that most of them work hard. But while many people in the world (including poor people) work hard too, it is clear enough to see that there is a wide margin between these sets of hard workers, what draws the margin between the rich and poor people is that the rich ones know how to work smart as much as they know how to work hard. Billionaires prioritize smart work over hard work. Other people may mistakenly see them as lazy people who like to sit idle and do nothing other than watch people work for them, but billionaires work with their minds than they work with their physical strength, which in turn makes all the difference.

A poor person thinks that he is maximizing and utilizing his resources when he does everything by himself. He is ignorant that doing so only limits his chances of expansion and stunts his growth. While there is nothing wrong with self-employment, referring to it as "owning a business" is a misnomer. When it comes to their job, billionaires understand that the concept of being a business owner means that their business can run without them. But poor people do what could be referred to as *self-employment*. Self-employment is a situation whereby the owner of a business is the one who is responsible for running every aspect of the business. What makes self-employment a poor approach to business is that nothing can work without the owner's presence and active engagement. The day the owner dies or encounters a serious physical, psychological, or spiritual challenge that incapacitates him, that is the day the business crumbles. Everyone cannot but watch how what he has worked hard to build crumbles without help.

More on OPM

OPM is an acronym for Other People's Money. Like the previous subheading, OPM was mentioned earlier in this book but will be further buttressed. This is a business model employed by every successful entrepreneur. Truth is, no business can grow and be sustained without leveraging on OPM. Many poor people start raising money for their business even before starting the business. They think that by trying to raise money for a business they have not started, they will have the advantage to scale quickly. Contrary to that, such businesses end up folding up in no time at all, that is one reason while billionaires don't do that. What they do is, they make sure that they start a business and grow it to a certain level before they scale. It is only after gaining social capital that they start asking for OPM. Apart from using other people's time (OPT), billionaires also know how to use Other People's Money (OPM). But billionaires only scale their businesses with OPM after gaining social capital. This is where many poor people miss it.

You can see this pattern with most prominent brands such as Tesla, Uber, Amazon, Microsoft, and many of the companies owned by billionaires. Before Dangote, Africa's richest man went public with his company, investors had understood his business model and were willing to put their money in it because the business had proven to be working. The owners of such companies only started using OPM in large quantities after they have gained social capital. People knew what the business was and understood the concept of the business. That way, many of the people who bought shares with them had already understood the *modus operandi* of the business.

As a rule, you need to only scale your business after running it for some time and achieving success. When you start your business, you want to first use whatever you have to test-run the business and grow it to a certain point before asking people to invest in it. That way, when you announce your intention to go public, investors will not hesitate to put their money in it because they understand that you have a business and your principles have proven to be working. In other words, you only scale your business after you have demonstrated the value of the business. The fact remains that no one can scale a business without using other people's money.

Billionaires have studied and mastered the art of scaling so much that when they do, people rush in to put their money there because they are confident that they are putting their money in something that has been demonstrated to be worthwhile over time. That way, even if such businesses eventually fail to yield profit as projected, investors do not become unnecessarily hard on themselves for being unwise, nor do they blame the business owners for playing a ploy on them. They would think that maybe something went wrong somewhere that was why the business model failed. That is what they will try to find out. They will not try to take the business owner to court unless there is clear evidence of recklessness and mismanagement of resources.

If you make the mistake of collecting people's money before starting your business and you are unlucky and the business fails, you ruin your reputation, and many will find it difficult to trust you in the future even if you bring up something that is legitimate. This is rampant amongst many poor people, the moment they have a business idea, the next thing they want to do is ask other people to give them a loan or invest in their idea. While there are certain investors like angel investors that may want to take a chance on such initiatives, the majority of investors only invest in businesses that have proven over time to be workable and to have a standard operational principle. However, in end, should the business fail, people may call you names and some may even take legal actions against you by labeling you a thief, scammer, or the likes. Remember, investors care about track records.

Here is a practical example: earlier on, I decided that I was not going to start raising capital for my real estate company until after we have successfully run the business for some time and built a name and credibility for ourselves. At that point, having demonstrated credibility and shown the world that we know what we are doing, we can scale and ask others to invest in our company. Right now, I can confidently say that we have already achieved that status. We have demonstrated that we know how to acquire a land in the right location. Since we have already built a structure and a brand and have become a multi-billion-naira real estate company in Africa if we decide to scale today and ask people to invest in our company, do you think anyone is going to be suspicious of our operations or doubt our credibility? Of course not, that exactly is the power of having a well-structured company before scaling your business with OPM.

CHAPTER SUMMARY

- Scaling a business means expanding the business and taking it to the next level.
- The two important things about scaling are understanding the law of timing and mastering the art of using other people's time and money.
- You must understand that investors do not invest in products, they invest in the business.
- When it comes to their job, billionaires understand that the concept of being a business owner means that their business can run without them.
- Billionaires have studied and mastered the art of scaling so much that when they do, people rush in to put their money there because they are confident that they are putting their money in something that has been demonstrated to be worthwhile over time.

PART SIXTEEN

EXPENDITURE CODE

Billionaires are disciplined spenders. They train themselves to spend their money strategically. But why be strategic about spending money? Why is that even important? Should anyone who has plenty of money think and worry about how much he spends? Aren't billionaires supposed to be people who are always buying what they want, going where they want, giving to whomever they please, and doing whatever they want with their money? Wrong. The fact is that billionaires do not spend their money pointlessly. They plan strategic expenditure. In the Expenditure Code, the spending patterns of billionaires are closely examined with practical examples. You'll see that they do not make money only to burn it!

The Expenditure Code is laid forth in two chapters. Chapter 25 examines the concept of *Budgeted Expenses,* which is a principle that plays a central role in the money management habits of billionaires. It examines the importance of budgeting for effectiveness and accountability. Chapter 26 analyses the concept of *Waste Avoidance.* It begins with the premise that billionaires detest waste. In other words, they do everything possible within their reach to see that their resources are not wasted. These are powerful principles that everyone who wants to generate and most especially *maintain* wealth must adhere to.

CHAPTER 25

BUDGETED EXPENSES

"Without budgeting, you misuse and waste money on trivial things."

– Dr. Stephen Akintayo

For the people who create wealth and maintain it, budgeting is a lifestyle. They budget for expenses such as clothes, food, gas for their car, charity donations, and all other recurring expenditures. Not only that, they also

"For the people who create wealth and maintain it, budgeting is a lifestyle."

allocate a certain amount of money for unforeseen circumstances outside their budget. Some call this their "Emergency Budget" or

"Emergency Account." In other words, billionaires have disciplined themselves not to spend money based on instincts or emotional pull; neither do they engage in spending money for spending sake. Everything that is to be spent is carefully budgeted with strict discipline. And that is one key component that differentiates rich people from poor people: discipline.

One of the perplexing and disheartening things I have observed with poor people is their lack of budgeting. It seems as if they become emotional as soon as some money enters their bank account. They just can't rest until all that money gets expensed! While rich people spend money based on legitimate needs, poor people spend theirs based on feelings. It is not uncommon to see poor people enter a store and start buying things not initially planned for. It would appear they spend without thinking. They allow their emotions to dictate and sometimes override their income limit. For billionaires, however, their expenditure must logically fit into their budget.

As I write this, I am lodging in a hotel and need some clothes. Generally, I only buy clothes twice a year, and I have a budget for that. For instance, if I intend to buy ten suits in a year, I first plan and budget for that accordingly. I don't shop for clothes by mistake or emotional appeal. It's not that I just go to one shop to sightsee and all of a sudden I'm on a shopping spree. Because I have budgeted my expenses for clothes for the entire year, I am not tempted by such things. So even though I'm currently in a city in Dubai, staying in a hotel that's attached to a shopping mall, I have only gone into the shopping mall twice. The first time was to watch a movie with my staff and the second time was to buy food. On each of those occasions, I went in, did what I planned to do, and got out without being sidetracked by the allures of beautiful clothes or the likes.

It is a matter of discipline to create and stick by a budget. It requires discipline because there are people who take the right step to budget their expenses, but because they lack discipline, halfway into the year they realize that they have already gone out of their budget because of certain "emergencies" or "contingencies" that weren't truly necessary. The fact is if you're not disciplined, even if you make a budget you may abandon it along the way. Therefore, it is important to not only make a budget for your expenses but to follow through and stick by it no matter what. This is the way billionaires think and act.

"The fact is if you're not disciplined, even if you make a budget you may abandon it along the way."

Plan Your Expenses

Life is full of temptations and appeals. Human wants are insatiable. We are always longing for something more. When something appeals to us, we immediately want to have it. If we don't get it with that sense of urgency and immediacy, we feel that we have been cheated, or we've not given ourselves what we *deserve*. And because of such insatiable desires, we often find ourselves spending money on things only to discover, after a short time, that those things do not satisfy us. We want newer or better versions of those things. And the quest for such things never ends. Advertisers and producers understand this secret about the human psyche and they seem to play on our emotions and succeed by such appeals. This is why they keep upgrading, changing, and introducing new products to the market to target the gullible and those who lack discipline. Copywriting is a major stream of income for many. What do copywriters do? Simply get you to buy, buy, buy, and buy some more, all the while believing that you *need* the product or service. It's emotional play. They simply appeal to your emotions, ego, and desires.

For you to escape the snares of making purchases at the slightest appeal, you must cultivate the discipline of planning your expenses. The saying that those who fail to plan are planning to fail couldn't be truer than in the area of financial management and budgeting. If you fail to plan your income and expenses, it will be difficult for you to acquire and maintain a fortune. You must be disciplined to not only put everything on paper but also ensure that you follow through and do what you have planned to do. Only what you have planned to do.

And this is one of the major mistakes poor people make. They find it difficult to track their income and expenses. Life just goes on. The result is constant complaints about lack and insolvency. The people who plan their income and expenses—no matter how little or much they get—are better off than those who fail to do so. Planning makes all the difference when it comes to the principle of financial management and wealth creation.

"If you fail to plan your income and expenses, it will be difficult for you to acquire and maintain a fortune."

Don't Succumb to Emergencies

A reason many remain poor is the mistake of allowing themselves to be pressured by friends, family and those in their inner circle who are always asking for financial help. Such pressure-applying people often present their financial needs as one form of emergency or another. Their requests for help may include things like taking care of a sick relative, support for their weddings, planning burial ceremonies, urgent school fees, and all kinds of things that may look genuine and authentic. The problem, though, is not so much about whether the case they present is genuine but whether you have planned for such things. The moment you allow people to put unnecessary pressure on you to meet their needs; you will find it increasingly difficult to build wealth.

Let me reiterate that I am not against anyone helping their family members, friends, and acquaintances with their financial obligations. My caution is to not allow yourself to succumb to unnecessary pressures that will constitute great financial burdens

> *"The moment you allow people to put unnecessary pressure on you to meet their needs; you will find it increasingly difficult to build wealth. "*

for you just because someone has played on your emotions and goodwill. The fact is that emergencies are unending—they will always arise. And giving money to solve one emergency is not a guarantee that the person you have helped or someone else will not approach you with the same kind of request in the coming weeks or months. The question is: How far can you go with that? Answer: Not far. Not far at all.

The people who put financial pressure on you and strive to make you feel as if you are responsible for their lives may not necessarily mean good for you. In fact, you may never satisfy them because they are always having one emergency or the other. You may be smart enough to save money but if you do not discipline yourself to resist the temptation of trying to solve everyone's problems, no matter the level of your income you may not be able to account for where your money goes. And that's how you stay stuck at one point, never advancing because the money goes out as soon as it gets in before you can even plan to put it to productive use.

"You may be smart enough to save money but if you do not discipline yourself to resist the temptation of trying to solve everyone's problems, no matter the level of your income you may not be able to account for where your money goes. "

I remember one time when a family member reached out to me asking for money. You know how those conversations usually start. They will first try to play the "sycophant game" on you by saying things like, "I thank God for your life."; "I have always known that you would be the star in our family."; "I have never doubted that you will be great."; "I have always known you are a good person"; "I have always known that you are going to be one of the richest people in our family."; "I know you have a good heart." And so on. On this occasion, the person greeted me very well. Of course, I knew what was going to come up after the wonderful compliments. The person continued, "You see, there's this problem I have, and it is an emergency." I simply replied, "First of all, I want you to know that I may be the MD/CEO of my company, but I am also an employee. Every month I too receive a salary like everyone else. And for the last month, I have exhausted my charity budget because a lot of people have asked me for money. So, you need to wait till next month when I receive my salary. I will consider you in my charity budget on my next pay."

"You must make people's emergencies bow down to your convenience. "

I wasn't mean but principled. And I kept to my words. Guess what? It turned out the emergency could wait for my convenience. Such is the principle you must imbibe if you want to create lasting wealth. You must make people's emergencies bow down to your convenience. While we understand that there are many contingencies in life and certain needs may require us from time to time to spend money that we have not planned for, the truth is most of the things we always refer to as emergencies can wait. The reason many people find it difficult to resist such requests is because they have not disciplined themselves to learn to say no. Learning to say no may cost you some friends, but you would be better off for it at the long run.

Since we know that people are generally difficult to please, why then must you always go the extra mile trying to please people by attending to all their financial emergencies? When people understand that you find it difficult to resist such requests, they will always come back with a different story. If you allow them to blackmail you because you have failed one time to meet their needs, you are in big trouble! If you mismanage your resources in trying to solve people's myriad problems, you will soon become broke, and the same people are going to call you a fool and dissociate themselves from you.

Learn to Budget

Budget is the gateway to financial management and accountability. Without it, you may work hard to earn money and still find yourself in a mess of financial woes. You must learn to budget all your expenses, including your charity donations. Remember, you are not the *Father Christmas* who is on a mission

Of giving everything you have. When people come to you and present a need, you must help them understand the principles with which you operate your finances. If your present budget does not warrant that, tell them that you currently don't have a provision for that in your budget but you will be glad to consider them next time.

Financial planning and budgeting go hand in hand. The reason many hesitate in making a budget is that they either think that budgeting is complicated or have the feeling that it is restrictive. But budgeting eases your burdens

> *"Financial planning and budgeting go hand in hand. "*

and makes you have a clear understanding of how you earn your money and, most importantly, how you spend it. You don't have to have an MBA or particularly love accounting to create a budgeting system. There are many free resources on the internet that can help you to create a simple budget.

People sometimes present the case of having little money as the reason they don't budget. They believe they don't require such discipline yet. But here's a simple, practical example that may resonate with some people. For a moment, let's consider the money that many poor people spend drinking beer. Most of such poor, beer-drinking folks would find it difficult to believe that the money they spend on a daily, weekly, monthly, and yearly basis to buy beer can build them a fortune. It may not make sense how a bottle of beer everyday might constitute fortune until you do the math. If you are a heavy beer drinker, you may be shocked to realize that the money you spend drinking beer in two to five years may be enough to build you a house. The same thing goes for some ladies who are shopping freaks. If you are a lady and you will give me access to your wardrobe, the money we might get after selling all your bags and shoes—that you hardly use—might be shocking to you. Let's not talk about the ones you buy for every wedding.

The point has been made: Start budgeting your expenses and you might just be on your way to building wealth. Without budgeting, you misuse and waste money on trivial things. Since you had no predetermined destination for the money, what's to keep it from rushing towards many places? If you refuse to imbibe this discipline, you have no right to be envious of your colleagues and acquaintances that do so and reap the dividends. Those who amass a fortune are people who decide to defy immediate gratifications by planning and budgeting their money. It makes sense to budget how you spend the money that you have toiled for. What does not make sense is working hard only to spend your hard-earned income on trivialities.

Prioritize Functionality over Luxury

A great principle I learned early on from one of my mentors is to learn to place functionality before luxury. In other words, while all work without play may make Jack a dull boy, play should never take precedence over work. In your financial planning, budgeting, and expenditure, you must see luxury as a reward for discipline and not the other way around. The moment you prioritize luxury

"It makes sense to budget how you spend the money that you have toiled for. What does not make sense is working hard only to spend your hard-earned income on trivialities. "

above your means of income, you are heading towards financial disaster. It does not mean that you should keep working hard without having time to enjoy the fruit of your labor, for doing so can be enervating and frustrating. However, if you make luxury your chief aim for hard work, it will be impossible to cultivate the discipline that will make you create riches and build wealth.

Using the example of beer, somebody may say, "But how much is a bottle of beer?" Let us do the calculation. The place to start is to ask how many bottles an average beer drinker takesin a week. Depending on your location and currency, by the time you calculate how much such a person spends in a year or two, you'd be shocked to realize how much heavy drinkers of beer spend annually and still remain poor. It is the little things that make the difference. The things that we often spend our monies on and take for granted are the things that make the difference.

In his bestselling book, *The Latte Factor,* which is written

> *"Always remember this: Your habits determine your decisions; your decisions determine your destiny. "*

in the form of a story, David Bach makes the case: The money most people spend in drinking coffee everyday can build them a fortune. Bach tries to show that *making* money is not as important as *keeping* it. In one of the conversations between Zoey (the main character) and the barista, the barista said, "The strange truth, Zoey, is that earning money—even outrageous amounts of money—does not necessarily lead to wealth. Why not? Because most people, when they earn more, simply spend more. Earnings are like the tide, you see, and your spending is like a boat. When the tide rises, the boat rises with it." I think you get the point!

Always remember this: Your habits determine your decisions; your decisions determine your destiny. Until you change your money habits, you are likely to remain where you are for a long time. Billionaires' wealth is a sum of their discipline in imbibing cardinal habits such as budgeting and planned expenditure. Think about people who have made great fortunes that you know. I amnot talking about people who do all sorts of illegal things to acquire riches and wealth. I am talking about legitimately wealthy people. What are their habits? Who are their friends? How do they spend their money, and on what? If you study billionaires, you will realize that all of them work with strict budgets, do a lot of financial planning, and are not carried away by frivolous expenses. Billionaires only spend money to get more money. You should read the last line again.

Here is a simple exercise that can help transform the way you spend your money. I want you to write down your expenses for one month. By this I mean, try to track down everything which you spend money on in a month, no matter how insignificant the amount may seem. If you follow this through, you will be amazed at the kinds of things that you spend most of your money on. And the second surprise may just be that those things are not very important. If you decide to cut off your expenses in those areas, you are already creating wealth for yourself; you're already simplifying your lifestyle.

Now that you've noted the things you spend your money on—the important things—proceed to confine yourself to that particular amount in the coming month. For example, for July, you find that you spent 20,000 naira on food. And from your analysis, you wouldn't likely eat more than 20,000 naira worth of food in a month. Now, make it a point that in the following month, you will not exceed 20,000 for food. Your friends could declare an all-evening eating spree at an expensive joint, humbly excuse yourself. Why? You have a budget to stick to.

Repeat the procedure for other areas of your expenditure besides food: clothing, airtime, data subscription, etc. After monitoring your likely expenditure on them in the initial month, set that amount as a ceiling—a ceiling you won't cross in the coming month. That's budgeting. And as we've discussed, sticking to it is as important as setting it. If for something remarkably pressing you overshoot your budget, forgive yourself and hold yourself accountable, purposing not to violate the budget again.

Meanwhile, you'll come to enjoy the feeling of being in control of your finances. And may even find that a simplified lifestyle, the one without unnecessary parties, raves and purchases, allows you focus your thoughts on avenues of creating value and wealth. It's more like declustering your wardrobe, so you can find room for what's necessary.

CHAPTER SUMMARY

- For the people who create wealth and maintain it, budgeting is a lifestyle.
- The fact is if you're not disciplined, even if you make a budget you may abandon it along the way.
- Billionaires' wealth is a sum of their discipline in imbibing cardinal habits such as budgeting and planned expenditure.
- Billionaires only spend money to get more money.
- Always remember this: Your habits determine your decisions; your decisions determine your destiny.

CHAPTER 26

WASTE AVOIDANCE

"To create riches and amass wealth, one must learn to avoid wasteful habits."

– Dr. Stephen Akintayo

One would think that because billionaires have a surfeit of money and wealth, they would naturally be wasteful; conversely, because poor people have very little, they would tend to be parsimonious. Unfortunately, the reverse often appears to be the case. Here is the paradox: Poor people have little, but tend to waste a lot; rich people have plenty and generally tend to avoid any form of waste.

"Poor people have little, but tend to waste a lot; rich people have plenty and generally tend to avoid any form of waste."

have plenty and generally tend to avoid any form of waste. Waste avoidance preserves wealth. Hardly would you meet someone who has become rich through legitimate means being wasteful. While they may not be miserly, billionaires know what it means to work hard and earn what they have, and they, therefore, hate any kind of wasteful attitude.

The most disastrous andreally unfortunate reason most poor people continue to remain poor from one generation to another is that they have not learned the principle of

> *"If what you are spending money on does not have any potential of generating more money for you, you are probably wasteful. "*

frugality. They are generally wasteful with the little they have. Someone once said that if you collect all the resources from the hands of every rich person in the world and give them to the poor, it would be a matter of time before the rich people get them back and the poor people return to their poverty. While this may sound hyperbolic, it points to the fact that until people learn to avoid waste, even if all the resources in the world are gathered and given to them, they will only waste them away.

Avoid Wasteful Habits

To create riches and amass wealth, one must learn to avoidwasteful habits. Wastefulness comes in different ways. For instance, some poor people want to compete with rich people in buying luxurious things just so they can feel important in society. They will buy expensive cars, expensive shoes, clothes, jewelry, phones, and the likes to impress people that don't even

"To create riches and amass wealth, one must learn to avoidwasteful habits."

care. That is wastefulness. Inthe end, because they live above their income, they end up accruing a lot of debt and spend their entire life feeling entangled by their wrong choices.

Let me give a practical example with some of the attitudes of poor people in my beloved country, Nigeria. Nigeria is said to be one of the poorest countries in the world based on poverty per capita. But at the same time, Nigeria is ranked as the country with the highest data purchases in the world. Nigerians buy airtime to make calls to the amount of over one trillion naira annually. A particular data even shows that Nigerians spend more money buying airtime than they spend on household items like food. And most disheartening of all, the majority of the people who purchase airtime are poor and most of the things they use their airtime and data to do are not business-related. They use them for social purposes, and even the social calls are mostly without reasonable purposes. This is a wasteful attitude that is informed by a poverty mentality.

The question is this: Why would poor people make more phone calls than rich people? What are they talking about? While rich people continue to build wealth on the data and airtime, poor people continue to waste the meager resources they have in buying airtime and data that do not bring any income to them. Can you see the irony? What I am saying is not guesswork. I have a company that sells airtime. I can remember how often I patronize the company. It is my company, but I don't buy airtime the way many poor people patronize my company.

If you want to become rich, you must discipline yourself to avoid such wasteful habits. If what you are spending money on does not have any potential of generating more money for you, you are probably wasteful.

Don't Patronize Laziness

Ceaselessly extending financial help to people discourages effort on their part. In Africa, people who are trying to succeed can easily be pulled down by their family members, relations, and friends. As soon as you begin to rise, people will start bombarding you with tons of needs and expect you to meet all of them. Because of such unrealistic expectations, many people usually get caught up in a web of trying to satisfy their kinsmen who present those needs and at the end of the day they become so overburdened that they find it difficult to rise

> *"If you keep giving people fish and fail to teach them how to fish, sooner or later you both will be without fish."*

and build wealth for themselves. The fact is that you are not helping people when you try to spoon-feed them. If you keep giving people fish and fail to teach them how to fish, sooner or later you both will be without fish. Many people, on the guise of trying to help, have made their family members and friends lazy and unproductive. You embolden people's laziness when you try to meet every one of their needs. A culture that encourages dependence at the expense of innovation is on a slippery slope.

We must put a stop to a culture where we continue to transfer poverty from one generation to the other on the guise of communal living—a *living* that encourages indolence and financial irresponsibility, where people do not understand how to make, manage, and multiply money. Many people don't have a basic understanding of money and its operations because these are not things that one learns within the formal school setting. Most people who love to earn and spend money have never read a book on financial management or financial intelligence. The majority of poor people have never met a billionaire who will teach them how to make, manage, and multiply money. Because of such ignorance, most poor people, even if they are educated, misuse their money and so continually remain poor. They become overburdened with credit card debt and all kinds of debts because of ignorance and lack of understanding of some basic principles about riches and wealth.

All my staffs know I abhor waste. You dare not waste anything around me. This is how serious it is when it comes to me detesting waste: I'd rather preserve my leftover food and use it the next day or give it to someone who needs it than put it in the trash. This is not because I am being unnecessarily miserly; it is because I hate waste. If someone comes visiting and is willing to eat the food, I will be happy to give it to them. It starts with such small things that may seem insignificant. But if you don't discipline yourself to start with such small and somewhat insignificant things, you will find it difficult to avoid waste when you have plenty. If you don't fight waste, you will die a poor person.Learn to see waste as an enemy that must be defeated.

Protect What You Have

Riches have wings. That is, they can fly away. Therefore, it is not enough to work hard to earn a fortune. You must know how to guard and protect what you have. Failure to protect the little you have opens it up to all forms of attacks. Money is sensitive and jealous. If it comes to you and you fail to protect and guard it, do not be surprised if you wake up someday and discover that it is all gone.

I always tell my staff anytime the income of my business goes down that it is a sign there is a waste going on somewhere. I must do everything possible to ascertain what the waste is and stop it before it costs me a fortune. Such is the attitude that you must have toward your riches. This is how billionaires think.

"If you don't fight waste, you will die a poor person.Learn to see waste as an enemy that must be defeated."

Billionaires take drastic measures to protect their wealth from all forms of attacks. They are constantly studying new market trends, looking for ways to multiply their wealth, and guarding all forms of attackers againstdevouring their possessions. In short, billionaires are acquainted with and play the money game well. Of what use would it be if after toiling if you allow either internal or external forces to devour what you have because of your carefree and careless attitude? Learn to guard what you have with the whole of your strength because it is worth the effort.

CHAPTER SUMMARY

- Poor people have little, but tend to waste a lot; rich people have plenty and generally tend to avoid any form of waste.
- To create riches and amass wealth, one must learn to avoid wasteful habits.
- If you keep giving people fish and fail to teach them how to fish, sooner or later you both will be without fish.
- Learn to see waste as an enemy that must be defeated.
- It is not enough to work hard to earn a fortune. You must know how to guard and protect what you have.

PART SEVENTEEN

LOVE CODE

Loving and succeeding at what you do requires a great deal of emotional strength. There are a lot of things that can drain a billionaire of emotional energy like setbacks, failures, resistance, and most of all, people. It is, therefore, important that the billionaire masters the skill of emotional intelligence in order for him to maintain his love for what he does and continue to get better results even in the face of hindrances and obstacles.

In the last chapter of this book, we will be looking at the role emotional intelligence plays in helping the billionaire deal with people (most especially) and other situations that could stand in the way of what he loves to do – making money.

CHAPTER 27

EMOTIONAL INTELLIGENCE

"People skill is one of the many advantages that billionaires have over others."

– Dr. Stephen Akintayo

Making money is a serious business that requires emotional strength and stability without which it is almost impossible to acquire and maintain wealth. In light of this, one of the skills that most rich people have is the ability to study and understand people so that they can maintain relationships that do not hamper their success.

Simply, to be wealthy, you must learn the skills of Emotional Intelligence. Emotional Intelligence (EI), or Emotional Quotient (EQ) as some like to refer to it, deals with the ability to study, understand, control, and evaluate emotions—yours and those of others.

". Just as making money can be learned, studying and understanding people is also a skill that can be learned through observation and practice."

While some people are naturally emotionally intelligent than others, this is a skill that can be learned. Just as making money can be learned, studying and understanding people is also a skill that can be learned through observation and practice. The amount of money you are likely to have and maintain depends to a great extent on your ability to understand and deal with people effectively.

People skill is one of the many advantages that billionaires have over others. Since money does not grow on trees, making money involves establishing and maintaining various kinds of relationships, some of which may be advantageous, and others may not. To be able to relate well with people, there is a need to understand their backgrounds, attitudes, where they are coming from, and their motives for doing what they do. If you lack this skill, either of two things will likely happen. First, you may either intentionally or inadvertently destroy certain relationships that are supposed to bring you good fortune. Secondly, you may fall prey to the hands of people who love to take advantage of others—people who love to play a psychological game on others to get what they want. You can't be in either of these situations and become wealthy. Hence, the need to have people skill so that you can understand both your friends and enemies and handle every situation with wisdom and tenacity.

"Billionaires engage in a lot of altruism, charity, and philanthropy. But they do so on their own terms."

Undeniably, emotions play an integral part in our lives and in our decision-making. They dictate and control the way we think, act, and make decisions about money. Hence, the need to develop the skill of interpreting, understanding, and responding to other people's emotions accordingly.

Don't Succumb to Emotional Blackmail

Many people have lost money because they succumbed to emotional blackmail by family members who will not manage their money but make a profession in manipulating, coercing, and cajoling others who do. They say things like, "Uncle I'm going to die if you don't send me money." I don't understand the logic behind such thinking. Or some people will say, "If you don't send me money today I am about to commit suicide." Those are empty threats by people who want to manipulate you and play all kinds of psychological games on you. They do so as a way of making you feel guilty for refusing to be responsible for them.

Billionaires don't fall victim to emotional blackmail from families, friends, and society. They understand this game so well that they are hardly moved by it. Does it mean that billionaires are cold-hearted and mean people who lack empathy? Absolutely not! Billionaires engage in a lot of altruism, charity, and philanthropy. But they do so on their own terms.

There was a day when one of my mentors was driving in his car and a beggar came begging for money. His driver pulled out a five hundred Naira note and gave it to the beggar. To their astonishment, the beggar took the five Naira, looked at it with anger and disdain as if to say, "Is this all you're going to give me?" And my mentor told his driver to collect the money from him. He inquired: Did he work for the money you gave him?

This is typically how some people will want to make you feel about what you have. Because they know that you are working hard and getting some money, they assume that they should have a good share of that money. When they want to ask you for help, they talk about outrageous amounts of money that leave you astounded. If you fail to meet their expectations, they become angry and resentful toward you as if you owe them something. Rich people don't become prey to such ruses and chicaneries.

Ignore the Trolls

Another thing that people do that is closely related to emotional blackmail is trolling. Trolls are in the habit of monitoring everything you do for the purposes of finding faults. Such people will want to make you feel guilty or ashamed of yourself at the slightest provocation. There are many trolls on social media. Unfortunately, because of lack of emotional intelligence, many people allow such trolls whom they may never know or have any relationship with, to taunt and bully them online. Let me give three examples to explicate this point.

The other day I took a picture while exercising and decided to post it online. Immediately, someone commented that I am living a lavish life instead of helping poor people. I saw that and thought to myself: How does exercising for my health relate to the poverty of another person? On another occasion, I took a picture on a business class in a commercial airplane. I said "commercial airplane" so that you can understand that I have not bought a private jet yet. Upon posting the picture

"Trolls are in the habit of monitoring everything you do for the purposes of finding faults."

on social media, someone started attacking me that I love showing off my wealth. I don't understand how taking a picture in a business class is a sign of showing off. The good thing about this incident was that immediately after posting that comment, some of my followers attacked the troll. One of them specifically posted the picture of Warren Buffett and Bill Gates in their private jets and inquired whether those could also be categorized as showing off.

Again, one day I had a haircut in Manhattan and afterwards went online to do a free training. I was talking about the principle of packaging; how normally in New York I could get a haircut for forty-five dollars in some neighborhood, but because I was in Manhattan, this was an expensive neighborhood and they charged me about two-hundred dollars for a haircut. Since I was talking about the power of packaging: how to package your business based on certain principles that must

"There are many people like that who make a job out of attacking others. When they notice that someone is living a happy life, it makes them sad."

be taken into consideration, I decided to use the example of my haircut to buttress my point. But not long after giving the example of my haircut, some people twisted the conversation upside down. There were more than 500 comments, most of them negative. Most people were complaining about how irresponsible I was to have such an expensive haircut. They said things like,"People are dying in Nigeria because of hunger and you are having a haircut for such an outrageous amount." Upon reading those comments, I thought to myself: For goodness sake, I am a private person. If you know that you don't want me to have a haircut that expensive, you should have bought a party ticket for me and asked me to contest the election using your money the way they do it in America. Since I am working hard and making money and can afford to have a good haircut, why shouldn't I? One of the trolls even went to the extent of saying that he once begged me for money and refused to give him, but I had the audacity to have such an expensive haircut.

There are many people like that who make a job out of attacking others. When they notice that someone is living a happy life, it makes them sad. Because they have many personal, unresolved conflicts and problems, they become bitter and resentful toward others who seem to be happy. Their aim is to see everyone failing, being melancholic and as angry as they are. Unfortunately, many people fall victim to such trolls.

Resist Spiritual Manipulation

Many poor people, especially in Africa, easily fall prey to spiritual manipulations by false prophets. While this is not a book that is meant to espouse and defend one religious or theological position against another, it is expedient that I mention this because it is one of the things that is holding many people back and making them perpetually poor in some parts of Africa. Here is a disclaimer: I am a religious person and don't have any problem with people giving money to advance the religious causes of their organizations. This is not what I am referring to here.

In Africa and some parts of the world, because of ignorance, many people spend their fortunes jumping from one prophet, seer, or fortuneteller to another looking for favor and trying to secure their future. Such false religious people have mastered the art of manipulation that they attract a lot of credulous followers who, in the guise of finding security, fall victims to their shenanigans, subterfuges, and sophistries.

I was once conversing with one of my mentees who is living in the United States while her mother is in Africa. She confided in me that her mother is always falling prey to spiritual manipulations by false prophets and seers to the point that her mother

> "Such false religious people have mastered the art of manipulation that they attract a lot of credulous followers who, in the guise of finding security, fall victims to their shenanigans, subterfuges, and sophistries."

was always bankrupt despite the daughter's good intentions and efforts in making sure that she constantly sends her money for the family's upkeep. She said, "My mother is always asking me for money. I will send her money but after a couple of days, she will call asking for more. I was baffled by the situation and decided to make some inquiries. It was then that I discovered that most of the money I send to her goes to some so-called prophets and seers who are always psychologizing and instilling fear in her about certain catastrophic events that are bound to happen to her or members of her family. In doing so, they extort all the money I send to her." This is one among many such sad, but true-life stories. Spiritual manipulation has become one of the most lucrative businesses in the world. By capitalizing on people's gullibility and ignorance, a lot of people have arisen, in the name of religion, extorting and robbing others of their fortunes.

But religious imposters and robbers find it difficult to manipulate billionaires through such gimmicks and chicaneries. The reason billionaires do not succumb to such deceits and duplicities by religious imposters is they have trained themselves to work hard for their money and understand human psychology. In other words, their emotional intelligence gives them an advantage over such so-called prophets. Therefore, they do not fall victim to their spiritual manipulations.

Develop a Thick Skin

On your way to the top, you will encounter many challenges and difficulties. One of the things you will constantly have to deal with is criticism. People are going to criticize for no just cause. They will accuse you of doing things that you are innocent about and call you all kinds of names. Such people forget the fact that as Dale Carnegie, author of one of the bestselling books of all time, *How to Win Friends and Influence People,* observed, "Criticism is futile because it puts a person on the defensive and usually makes him strive to justify himself. Criticism is dangerous because it wounds a person's precious pride, hurts his sense of importance, and arouses resentment." Carnegie went on to say, "By criticizing, we do not make lasting changes and often incur resentment."

> *"Billionaires listen to opposing views and learn from them. But they do not allow themselves to be traumatized by enemies and haters who are out to mar their reputation or guilt them."*

To handle people who specialize in vitriol and putting others down, you must develop a thick skin. Developing thick skin does not mean being nonchalant about the concerns of others. It means having the emotional intelligence to know where people are coming from and the wisdom to handle them appropriately.

Billionaires listen to opposing views and learn from them. But they do not allow themselves to be traumatized by enemies and haters who are out to mar their reputation or guilt them.

CHAPTER SUMMARY

- Making money is a serious business that requires emotional strength and stability without which it is almost impossible to acquire and maintain wealth.
- Emotional Intelligence (EI), or Emotional Quotient (EQ) as some like to refer to it, deals with the ability to study, understand, control, and evaluate emotions—yours and those of others.
- Billionaires don't fall victim to emotional blackmail from families, friends, and society.
- Billionaires do not succumb to deceits and duplicities by religious imposters because they have trained themselves to work hard for their money and understand human psychology.
- Billionaires listen to opposing views and learn from them. But they do not allow themselves to be traumatized by enemies and haters who are out to mar their reputation or guilt them.

Printed in Great Britain
by Amazon

43137728R00195